# LEAVE A
# LIGHT ON

Simon Jackson

**First Published 2020**
Cadogan Press

**ISBN: 978-1-8380073-1-7**

Set and designed by Cadogan Press
Printed by Book Printing UK

*For Sophia*

*"If you can dream it, you can do it."*
Walt Disney

# ABOUT THE AUTHOR

Simon has taught in London schools since 1993 and has been a head teacher since 2011. An experienced leader of training for university students, NQTs, middle and senior leaders, he is also a serving coach and school inspector. Passionate about the importance of the Early Years and the expressive arts within education, these elements are at the heart of his educational philosophy. Unsurprisingly, he's also passionate about developing leadership capacity at all levels.

Simon lives with his wife, Laurielle (also a school leader) and daughter Sophia in London. He's happy when Arsenal have won, and the Guinness is good.

Simon Tweets @sjacksonAFC
Website: primaryvedette.com

# CONTENTS

# Foreword

I first met the leadership dynamo that is Simon Jackson after speaking at a conference for headteachers that had been organised by Lambeth Local Authority down in Brighton. Simon came up to chat about the presentation I had given and asked if I would be willing to work with his school and other local church schools in his network. That was over four years ago, and the rest is history.

It has been a privilege and a delight to work with senior and middle leaders from across this group of primary schools, sharing with them my own leadership learning journey, often trying out new ideas for conferences or publications.

Throughout this process, I have come to realise that Simon, too, is an avid reader of leadership books and articles. But he has also been a truly inspiring leader within his own organisation. Anyone visiting St Leonards doesn't need Ofsted or SIAMS to know they are in an extraordinary school.

For a while now I have been encouraging (perhaps badgering!) Simon that he should share his own leadership learning journey. When he decided to do this through the lens or framework of my own book, Leadership Matters, I could not have been more flattered or delighted.

What he has created is a thoughtfully curated set of leadership reflections that do far more than just tell the story of St Leonards' success, impressive as that is. This book is a very human, compassionate book about how leaders can galvanise teams to create community in a powerful, empowering and loving way. Never has this been more important than it is today.

**Andy Buck**
Founder of Leadership Matters

# Introduction

*"Happiness can be found, even in the darkest of times, if one only remembers to turn on the light."*
**Albus Dumbledore**

The cupboard under the stairs in our house is very much like Harry Potter's at number 4, Privet Drive. Some two and a half years after moving to our home, I went to return the iron to the shelf within the cupboard, something which I'd done well over a hundred times before. However, on this occasion due to clumsiness, I overshot the end of the shelf and the iron stand clattered into the wall beyond it. Out of nowhere, a light came on which illuminated the entire cupboard. A light that I never knew had existed…and I had never looked for it.

The concept of light is synonymous with truth and hope. For people of faith, it of course holds additional significance. However, it is to be expected that, in most situations, if there is a light to be seen it will be easy to notice. In the years since I became a head teacher, I've learned that whilst there are definitely some amazing people whose light is there for all to see, there are others whose light is no less bright but is sometimes less obvious to notice and needs revealing.

*leadership about how your light can illuminate others and you drawing from others*

I should make it clear from the outset, that though this book often contains my personal perspective, it is not about personal glory or advancement. It is about how your light can illuminate the way for others. It is about how you can draw on the light coming from others. It is about how as a team you can nurture each other for the benefit of all within an organisation. Ultimately, it's about how you can find a way to reveal the brilliance of what takes place within your school so that all children and staff may be able to shine.

*yes*

I will refer closely to the Leadership Matters model created by Andy Buck. I will draw on the experience of my own leadership journey and explore these concepts through the medium of light. The setting for this journey is St Leonard's Church of England Primary School in Streatham, London. Now a member of the Southwark Diocesan Board of Education's Multi Academy Trust (SDBEMAT), it's a school with over 200 years of history that we'll explore later.

This book is intended to be accessible and relevant to all. As such, to my Church school leader colleagues, I acknowledge that there are many occasions in this book when the foundation of a leadership concept is not developed to its theological potential. There is, however, an epilogue at the back of this book containing some material linked to each chapter that you may find useful when reflecting personally or discussing elements of this book with your colleagues from a Christian perspective. To those of other faiths and none, whilst I invite you to take an interest in the epilogue, it is not essential to developing your understanding of our leadership journey or in applying the Leadership Matters model to your own situation. In sharing my experience, I hope not only to be an articulate ambassador for Leadership Matters but also to give you encouragement and affirmation within your own setting and from your personal perspective.

The Leadership Matters model has four broad elements: Personal Qualities, Your Situation, Leadership Actions and Leadership Approach. Brilliant in their simplicity when one reads them, they naturally become more complicated when the human

*The Leadership Matters (Andy Buck) approach*

dimension is added. Hopefully, this book will help you to see the light as well as prepare you for those inevitable periods of darkness. As Aristotle said, "It is during our darkest moments that we must focus to see the light."

May I direct you to the acknowledgments at the end of this book. *Leave A Light On...Why Your Leadership Matters* is truly the result of so many wonderful people who I'm blessed to have known or worked with.

There is, however, one person whom I must mention at the start of this book because the moment I met him was the moment that this book became a possibility. I first met Andy Buck at a Local Authority head teachers' conference in the spring of 2016. I was captivated by the uniqueness of his content, by the fact that he didn't once mention anything about the inspectorate or government. He was just an authentic, gracious and knowledgeable leader focused on appealing to the hearts and minds of people. I knew I'd met someone whom I could learn from. Four years later, I'm still learning and I'm loving every minute of it.

This book spans almost a decade of leadership development. The first half of the decade certainly laid the foundations and paved the way, but it's worth noting that since the school adopted the Leadership Matters model, we've achieved increased success in a variety of ways. It is Andy who has personally encouraged me to write this book and has guided me through the process. For this, I am both honoured and extremely grateful.

# Preface

*"Purpose is the reason you journey. Passion is the fire that lights the way."*
**Unknown**

### Background

I have been using the *Leadership Matters* approach as a head teacher for four years. Each teacher at St Leonard's receives a copy of the book either at the beginning of their second year if they join as an NQT or on joining the school as an experienced practitioner. Our senior leadership team often hold book club sessions as part of our weekly meetings where we discuss existing challenges in the light of this model. We subscribe to the *Leadership Matters* website and use its tools, videos, templates and articles extensively to support leadership development for our middle and senior leaders. Andy is a regular visitor and supports our local cluster of Church schools. As such, I have had some great experience on which to draw for the content of *Leave A Light On.*

## Structure

This book is intended to complement the *Leadership Matters* model. It has four elements to it. Three are interwoven throughout the book and one is contained separately within the epilogue. Firstly, there is relevant information from Andy Buck's original book for you to refer to at key points. I also explore how the approach may look in practice within the context of a primary school. At the end of each chapter, there are questions for you to reflect on or to discuss with your colleagues. The epilogue will be of particular relevance to leaders in Church of England schools and offers reflection on each chapter from the perspective of Christian leadership.

## Purpose and Passion

The purpose of this book is simple. I wish to explain how the *Leadership Matters* approach has informed my leadership, transformed our school and inspired a new group of leaders to adopt this approach. I hope that it will resonate with you in some way so that you can also have confidence in the benefits of adopting the methodology. Ultimately, I wish to see *Leadership Matters* considered as a movement that promotes the very best in school leadership so that each reader of this book feels that they can make progress on their own leadership journey.

I also wish to include the perspective of a Church school leader. Approximately one million children attend Church of England schools. About 15 million people alive today went to a Church of England school and a quarter of primary schools have a Church of England foundation. As such, to consider *Leadership Matters* within such a context is too good an opportunity to turn down.

I hope that by reading *Leave A Light On,* you will reflect on how your own leadership can develop and for what purpose you've been called to serve. If this book helps you to invest time thinking about yourself as a leader rather than a manager of data, budgets and staffing issues, then I will have achieved something.

# 1

# Stand for Something

"*Nothing can dim the light that shines from within*"
**Maya Angelou**

It all starts with you. The Leadership Matters model begins by calling you to look at your personal qualities. In his book, Andy Buck states, "*For all leaders, having a strong sense of one's own personal characteristics is a hugely powerful and affirming base from which to lead, particularly when the challenges of a school leadership role have the potential to become all-consuming.*"

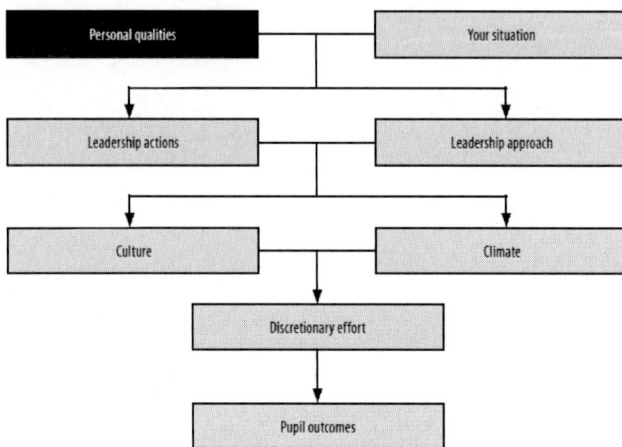

| Personal qualities | | Your situation |
| Leadership actions | | Leadership approach |
| Culture | | Climate |
| | Discretionary effort | |
| | Pupil outcomes | |

## Knowing yourself

Our school senior leadership team's way into the Leadership Matters approach was through its LM Persona tool available on the Leadership Matters website. This online tool asks just 20 questions in order to create a detailed predisposition report for any school leader. Based on a Jungian analysis of personality, the tool is designed to help leaders better understand their natural strengths, ways of working and potential areas for growth.

There are four pairs of personality characteristics at the heart of Jung's theory:
*Extroversion (E) or Introversion (I)* – whether you are energised and take pleasure from the outer world or from your inner self
*Sensing (S) or Intuition (N)* – relying on the recognised senses or on your own interpretation and imagination for the future
*Thinking (T) or Feeling (F)* – Making judgments based on logic and rules or based on your own feelings and those of others
*Judging (J) or Perceiving (P)* – Preferring things to be decided or being open to new possible options and outcomes

My overall personality type is ENTJ and I've been told that I'm classically so! The LM Persona tool reassuringly offers far more information about one's natural strengths than character imperfections. At the head of the report, it offers a three-point summary – two strengths and one gently worded aspect for consideration. I'm going to begin by illuminating the latter so that my profile can end on a positive note!

I am so glad that I've read Steve Munby's book, *Imperfect Leadership* (2019). In it he states that, *"imperfect leadership should be celebrated."* That's just as well for me! My biggest flaw (let's call it out for what it is) was revealed thus: *"You might benefit from being a bit less direct with people sometimes."* Anyone who knows me will testify that this assessment is mildly and generously worded.

As the saying goes, "A clever person knows what to say; a wise one knows whether to say it or not." There are occasions when I've been left to reflect on the fact that I've been clever but lacking in wisdom. In addition to this, whilst I know that I'm a loyal friend, I'm also not inhibited in the slightest at the prospect of having an adversary. Years' ago whilst doing my NPQML training, I opened up about these aspects of my character to the trainer. What she said I've never forgotten. *"Simon – you just need to learn to respond rather than react."* The simplicity and yet the enormous implications of this advice left me stunned. The subtle difference between the two words not only relates to the tone used but also the time taken to think before words are expressed. Have a think about yourself for a moment. Are you predisposed to responding or reacting? Under what circumstances are you most likely to respond or react?

Some twenty years or so later, I'm still trying to respond more often than I react. I still fail on many occasions both personally and professionally but, as we'll explore later when I look at how our team was created, I have certain members of the senior leadership team who are brilliant at disarming me. Their very presence can quickly save me from either a self-inflicted wound or from arousing resentment in others. When their face appears at the door and their opening gambit is, *"Are you ok?"* I'm

when to speak – when to hold your tongue.

immediately alerted to the prospect that I may at the very least be coming close to making a wrong move. Ronald Reagan famously said, *"When you can't make them see the light, make them feel the heat."* This is my natural predisposition but, as the title of this book would suggest, I recognise that as a whole school leader, employing the former strategy is more desirable and far more likely to be successful. As such, I'm eternally grateful (as I'm sure my colleagues are!) to those selfless individuals who maintain the equilibrium and sustain me with an encouraging word or simply a look on occasions.

Before I go too far and paint myself out to be some psychotic despot prowling the corridors ready to explode at any given moment, I will also, as an act of mitigation, share a couple of the positive aspects of my LM Persona report. It states: *"You are naturally someone who others look to for leadership"* and *"You will usually be decisive, clear sighted and authoritative".*

I hope that, having read the paragraphs above, you now feel that you know enough about me as a leader, that it hasn't put you off from reading the rest of the book and that you can begin to reflect on what may be brought into the light within your own profile.

## Knowing each other

As a senior leadership team (SLT), I would encourage you to openly share your personality profile results – the headlines at least. There are two main reasons for this. Most importantly, you will be able to see whether or not you have a good blend of personality types represented on your team, remembering that the primary purpose of the SLT is to enable and develop your whole organisation; it shouldn't exist in a vacuum. Secondly, it can be a great ice-breaker and makes for a great first conversation about Leadership Matters. When we shared our profiles at our SLT meeting, we were able to laugh at our individual areas for development. We didn't take ourselves too seriously and recognised that these profiles contained far more truth than fiction. This fostered a sense of honesty, transparency and acceptance. Above all, it reassured us that, as a result of us all, whole school leadership was strong. The whole premise behind Leadership Matters is that no single personality type is more predisposed to be successful than another. For example, whilst I'm most definitely an extrovert, one only has to read Jamie Thom's *A Quiet Education (2020)* to understand the huge benefits that can be realised from having an introvert as a leader. The important thing is to be self-aware of both one's positive and less well-developed characteristics and then to play to one's strengths whilst utilising the strengths of others. You may wish to consider the Johari window (Luft and Ingham 1955) below and referred to in the self-awareness and predisposition section of Leadership Matters book to assist you with this.

|  | Known to self | Not known to self |
|---|---|---|
| **Known to others** | **OPEN** | **BLIND SPOT** |
| **Not known to others** | **HIDDEN** | **UNKNOWN** |

*Open*, characteristics that are known by you and others.
*Hidden*, characteristics that are known by you but which you do not reveal to others.
*Blind spot*, characteristics others know about you, but you do not know about yourself.
*Unknown*, characteristics that are not known to you or others.

The Leadership Matters model looks at three other important factors relating to your personal qualities: *Emotional Intelligence; Courage and Resilience; Humility*

## Emotional Intelligence

Daniel Goleman's model (2000) above explains how he believes emotional intelligence begins with better self-awareness.

This in turn supports one's awareness of others and provides an opportunity for you to manage your own emotions.

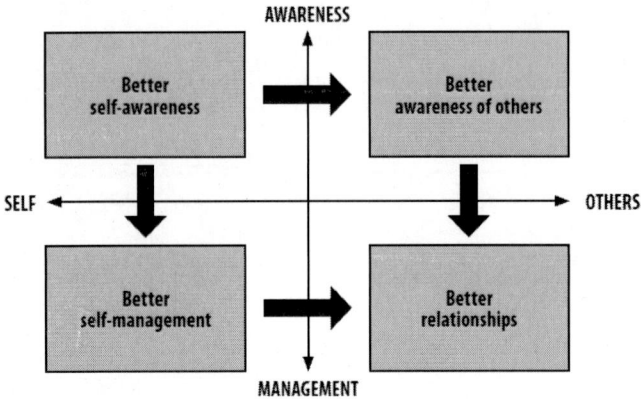

Together, the combination of these two provide the basis by which one is able to build better relationships, which is critical for any leader.

## Courage and Resilience

Leadership Matters refers to a model for resilience developed by an organisation called Robertson Cooper. They believe there are four key dimensions to resilience, as shown in the diagram below.

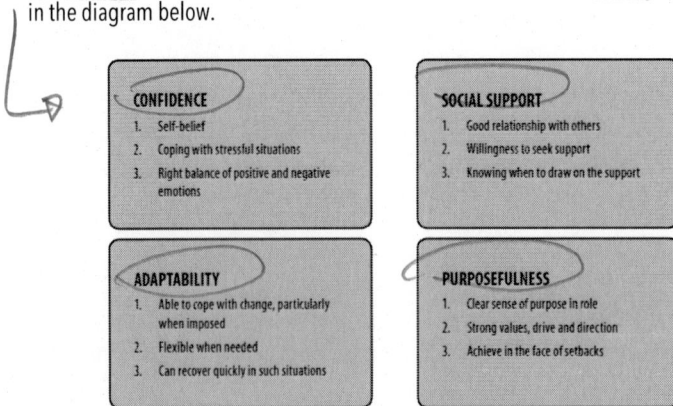

**CONFIDENCE**
1. Self-belief
2. Coping with stressful situations
3. Right balance of positive and negative emotions

**SOCIAL SUPPORT**
1. Good relationship with others
2. Willingness to seek support
3. Knowing when to draw on the support

**ADAPTABILITY**
1. Able to cope with change, particularly when imposed
2. Flexible when needed
3. Can recover quickly in such situations

**PURPOSEFULNESS**
1. Clear sense of purpose in role
2. Strong values, drive and direction
3. Achieve in the face of setbacks

Andy Buck identifies several characteristics which are important for a leader to develop in relation to resilience. *Resilience*

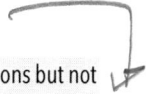

- ∞ Manage your emotions - The important thing is to recognise your emotions but not be governed by them
- ∞ Turn negativity into positivity - If you can soak up criticism, show you are listening, prove to others that you want to adapt, improve and learn, then you can turn negative situations into positive ones
- ∞ Stay optimistic - Staff look to leaders in school for reassurance when things are difficult. They need to see leaders being optimistic, however hard this is to do, to make them feel secure in difficult or uncertain circumstances
- ∞ Learn and improve from criticism – find the time and space to quietly reflect on criticism, using the help of a colleague if necessary
- ∞ Keep going - schools don't become outstanding overnight. It is the culmination of hard work over a significant period of time
- ∞ Take calculated risks – we'll look at this in the chapter *Sailing West*

## Humility

The main point here is that as a school leader you are focused on being ambitious for your school rather than yourself. This links back to the importance of moral purpose, more about which you can read in the epilogue.

## Using your intuition to lead with conviction

As leadership begins with your personal qualities, in its earliest phase, it's also established through vision. In our school's case my predisposed nature for having a clear vision, seeing the big picture and relying on intuition was well supported by the qualities and characteristics of the wider leadership team. Therefore, when looking at the Personal Qualities section of Leadership Matters, it's important to do so with the aim of developing others as well as oneself.

If you are in the role of head teacher, your ability to have and to articulate a clear and exciting vision is going to be vital in raising the chances of whole school success. You also need to be able to transfer that personal passion into the hearts and minds of others.

Two complementary characteristics which I believe to be important for this purpose are intuition and conviction. Intuition is not merely a visionary hunch. It is also driven by belief. I fear that these characteristics in their purest forms are becoming less visible as the level of school accountability increases within our education system. I also think that our approach and response to educational research needs realigning.

Let me preface what I'm about to say by acknowledging that research in all aspects of life is vitally important. It will be as a result of research that many medical conditions will hopefully be overcome. It will be as a result of research that new technologies will be developed, and hopefully natural disasters will become less frequent. Research can be hugely beneficial, and many action research projects are worth participating in. My concern is that within education, some research is politically motivated rather than genuinely commissioned with a desire to break new ground. Politicians may rely on research, sometimes not even really exploring beyond the headline outcomes or questioning its origin because it suits a political narrative. They are looking for standardised global solutions to complex localised problems and they are enforcing strategies without thinking about context. When it comes to your leadership situation, just remember the adage that sometimes, when you follow the masses, the "m" is silent!

At the very least, we should question the word "independent" when it's applied to published research and its associated data. For example, consider the Program for International Student Assessment (PISA) statistics that are produced every three years and publicised widely in the media. I won't list all my objections to them here but our work in schools is often too heavily judged by national performance in these tables.

Let's just acknowledge that anything that's named as PISA may have dodgy foundations and a tendency to lean heavily in one direction!

For leadership to be authentic it has to come from within the individual. You cannot always be sure that your efforts will be successful, but you cannot always wait for evidence to support your instinct. We have to have faith in ourselves as leaders and in our teams. If all we ever do is based on something which others have done before, where is the new learning? Where is the personal and organisational growth? Where is that hope for a better tomorrow?

As the saying goes, *"if you don't stand for something, you'll fall for anything."* I am not advocating being blind to reason and disrespecting the wisdom of others, but no amount of research is going to persuade me, for example, to abandon my belief that Early Years Foundation Stage is the top priority when developing high quality provision within a primary school, nor will it persuade me to believe that the expressive arts are anything less than vitally important within our schools and wider society.

*Good example*

My desire for you as a school leader is that you lead with conviction, that you have faith in yourself and your team, that you lead for the benefit of others, that you light the path for all those who share your conviction and embolden them to carry that light forward. As such, take time to reflect on your personal qualities before reading the next chapter.

These questions may prove helpful.
Why do you wish to lead?
What do you believe to be your best leadership qualities?
What desirable characteristics are less well developed?
How will you lead with conviction?
What do you stand for?
What will you fight for?
Who sustains you?

*Key Q's.*

# 2

# In the Beginning

*"We're absolute beginners with eyes completely open but nervous all the same"*
**David Bowie**

Having looked at yourself as deeply and as honestly as you can, this chapter is going to encourage you to look outwardly, to be able to see both the light and the shadows within your leadership context. The Leadership Matters model requires you to be able to bring your personal qualities to bear upon the situation you are faced with and for you to be able to make an accurate assessment of that situation before acting upon it. We will look at how to begin in a new situation as well as how to approach situations from an experienced position.

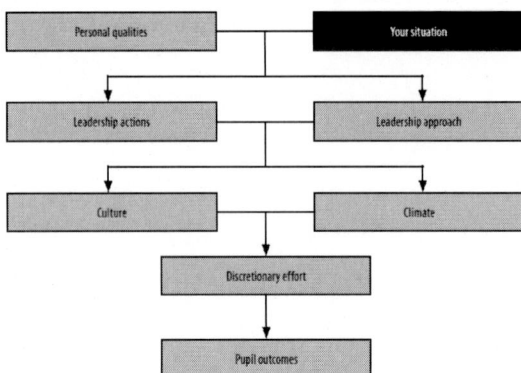

| Personal qualities | Your situation |
| Leadership actions | Leadership approach |
| Culture | Climate |
| Discretionary effort |
| Pupil outcomes |

## A New Situation

Taking up a headship, no matter how much training and preparation one's had, is like visiting a foreign destination for the first time. Even though you've seen the attractive pictures of it online or in a brochure and people have told you that it's a great place, it's not until you're there that you can begin to understand the culture and adjust to the climate. Taking the time to acclimatise is really important, because if one enters into the heat without the necessary caution, preparation and protection, one can quickly get sunburnt!

This being said, it is important that you are also as open as you feel able. For example, I had shared with the entire staff team on day one of my headship that, to give them a head start on their journey of "working me out" the only two things which "wound me up" were untidiness (in people or places) and lateness. I explained that, as long as people didn't transgress in these two areas, everything else could be worked out through the process of getting to know each other. By doing something like this when beginning in your role, you are both showing a little vulnerability by sharing something about your personality, as well as establishing a couple of basic standards and showing a willingness to empathise with the feelings of staff.

I was fortunate that my headship began at the beginning of a summer term. This meant that I had a whole term before the new academic year began to keep my eyes open and identify the bringers of light as well as those from the dark side. It gave me time to gain an understanding of what our situation involved academically, socially, emotionally, spiritually and financially before having a summer break to reflect on what I'd learned.

There may be many factors involved when considering whether you first see the light or the shadows within your working context. LM Persona may have revealed that you're naturally predisposed to focus on a perceived problem or indeed a possibility. You may be experiencing a particularly positive or challenging period in your personal life. Such factors can potentially cloud your judgment when approaching new situations.

Alternatively, the situation you find yourself in may indeed be so obvious, that the major changes required are easier to see even if the specific route ahead is not yet illuminated. Jarlath O'Brien uses the analogy of asking yourself whether you're required to move the piano or to play it.

I would imagine that, if you're beginning in a new context and your school has a journey to make, you're almost certainly going to be involved in some moving before the Beethoven in you comes galloping to the fore!

## Quick Wins

The Leadership Matters book refers to a school development model by Sir David Carter (see below). It has four steps: De-Clutter, Repair, Improve and Sustain. We will look at the first two elements as part of this chapter and they were certainly pertinent to the situation at St Leonard's in 2011.

| DE-CLUTTER | REPAIR | IMPROVE | SUSTAIN |
|---|---|---|---|
| School broken | Control from chaos | Leadership more pro-active | Maslow's self actualisation |
| No under-pinning of the future | Reactive decision-making | Strategies start to embed | Growth of confidence and innovation |
| Real truths begin to emerge as project unfolds. | Making feel like a normal | Outcomes never as bad again | Begin taking calculated risks |

Identifying quick wins is as important as having more long-term ambitions for the organisation. Whilst the de-cluttering stage of the model is not intended to be taken literally, this was actually the case for us, because the school environment itself needed significant improvement. Our quick win arrived in the form of a skip. Several skips to be truthful. Though the launch of the clear up was almost immediate, the actual time it took ran into a few years!

There is a serious point to be made. Along with standards of behaviour (from both adults and pupils), environment is key when it comes to enabling learning to take place. By focusing on improving the environment so that adults can teach and children can learn in better conditions, it gives more time for one to gain an understanding of the people within the organisation.

Therefore, "The Great Clear-Up" (as it has jokingly since been referred to by the staff involved) provided an impetus for a new era to begin. People could see improvement, they could feel momentum building, but they hadn't been challenged to improve or change themselves...yet!

**Emerging Truths**

The de-cluttering stage of Carter's model identifies when a school is broken, having no underpinning of the future and being in a situation where real truths begin to emerge. Some or all of this may or may not resonate with you. For example, it would have been too harsh to describe St Leonard's as being broken when I took up my headship. It was true, however, that certain important relationships were indeed broken and, as a result, there was not a stable underpinning of the future in place. As the early days of my headship unfolded, real truths did begin to emerge about the quality of teaching, curriculum and assessment in particular. In your own situation, it's important that, though you may be nervous, you keep your eyes completely open.

As well as any quick wins you may have achieved, you need to find out not only where excellence already exists, but also where there are people who are "on board" as early adopters and supporters of your leadership.

## Behaviours and Values

The performance, behaviours and values section of the Leadership Matters model is highly useful when trying to gain an understanding of the situation regarding the individuals involved within your setting. The Pendleton and Furnham model (2012) illustrated below, demonstrates how behaviours, values and performance can be judged and worked on within the staff team.

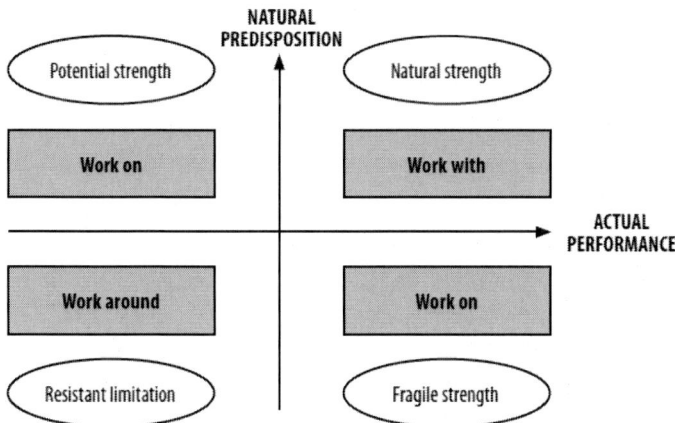

For areas where an individual has *natural strengths*, it's important to give them the chance to improve further and excel, so that they become the expert within your team or organisation for that particular area.

*Potential strengths* are those areas which, with just a little attention, a colleague could be great at. This is generally because they have a predisposition towards it and just need to give it some focus or fine tuning.

*Fragile strengths* are things that an individual can do well if they put their mind to it, but success doesn't come naturally or easily. For example, all school leaders need to be able to use data effectively. For some, this will be a natural strength. For others, it takes practice and focus. But it is achievable.

In contrast, what the model calls *resistant limitations* are those things an individual is neither good at nor interested or motivated to try to improve at. Pendleton and Furnham argue that rather than persisting to make this a focus for development, one is much better trying to find a workaround, which usually involves finding someone else to do it. It should be said, however, that some things can't be offloaded. One can't have a teacher for example who is unable to manage a class or create a culture of good behaviour within it.

### Managing differential performance in others

As well as knowing about how others prefer to work and playing to their strengths, the very best leaders in schools, at all levels, are good at knowing how well colleagues in their team are performing and respond accordingly. Pendleton and Furnham (2012) have developed an interesting model (below) which suggests leaders can group colleagues according to the behaviours and values of others and their performance at work.

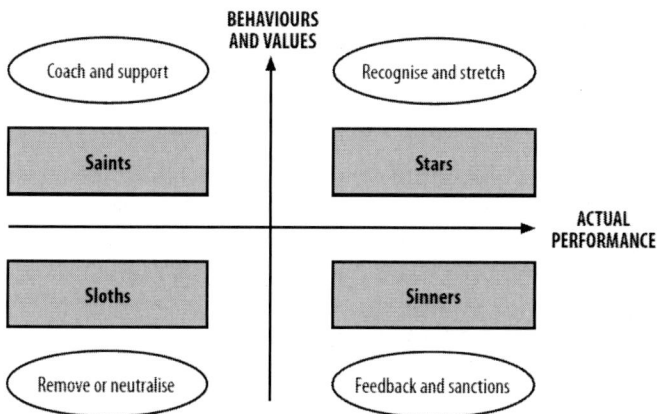

```
                          BEHAVIOURS
                          AND VALUES

  ( Coach and support )      ↑    ( Recognise and stretch )

  ┌──────────────┐           │    ┌──────────────┐
  │    Saints    │           │    │    Stars     │
  └──────────────┘           │    └──────────────┘
                                                              ACTUAL
────────────────────────────┼──────────────────────────→  PERFORMANCE

  ┌──────────────┐           │    ┌──────────────┐
  │    Sloths    │           │    │   Sinners    │
  └──────────────┘           │    └──────────────┘

  ( Remove or neutralise )        ( Feedback and sanctions )
```

Andy Buck describes *Stars* as, *"your high performers who are doing a great job"* and work in a way that is absolutely in line with the desired culture and climate. You need to be careful not to take these fantastic individuals for granted or forget to prioritise their needs on occasions. Just like you, they need to be challenged, stretched and recognised for what they do.

The more they feel they have a say in their future, the better, but you need to make sure you don't over promise. They will usually appreciate development opportunities, whether formal or informal. *Stars* are potentially brilliant coaches.

*Sloths* are at the opposite end of the spectrum. These are individuals who are performing poorly and are potentially undermining your culture and climate. You need to quickly understand what sits behind their poor outcomes and attitude and give them very clear and unambiguous feedback about what needs to change in relation to both. Make it clear they are making choices about their future. They then need to improve very quickly or there will be consequences. Ultimately, you need to be prepared to work out a way for them to leave the school.

*Saints* are committed and always do their best to deliver the goods. They're just not very good at delivering them. Because of their effort and behaviour, you need to make sure they are supported and coached in order to have the chance to improve. If they do so, you should continue to support them. Only if, after sustained support, they are still not able to perform to the required standard, should these people also be encouraged to *seek new opportunities elsewhere.*

*Sinners* provide the most frustrating challenge of all because these are capable practitioners. However, they behave in a way that undermines the culture and climate you are trying to establish. They often pay mere lip service to agreed school policy and initiatives because *their* way is better, or they don't need the additional structure to assist them. They are often disloyal about your leadership and others in the wider team. In short, they are the people that can drain your soul on sight. The effect of such people is not on standards but on morale. As such, rather than coaching, they need to be given very clear feedback about what needs to change and by when. They must change their behaviour and attitude or face the consequences. It is a blessed relief when these people leave!

With all of these groups, they should be responded (not reacted) to in order to improve their behaviour or performance. I have found this model to be really useful during leadership team meetings. A good exercise to undertake without having the need to discuss individual members of staff, is to consider what each of the four person types would actually look like (behaviourally, not physically) in your school and to consider the impact of this upon each of you within the leadership team and on the organisation as a whole. Andy Buck concludes that the intention isn't for us as leaders to place staff in one of the boxes. However, I'd be lying if I said that I hadn't done so…on several occasions!

Let's be honest, even with those whom we find it more difficult to warm to, we want them to succeed for the benefit of the children at least. In using this model, when you do have to apply it to a member of staff, you can dispassionately break down the behaviours and issues involved and then decide on which member of the team is most likely to be successful in achieving the desired change or outcome through having a conversation with the member of staff involved. In the first instance, the person selected to respond should be decided based upon personality rather than hierarchy.

## Repair or Replace

The repair stage of Carter's model involves you establishing control from chaos, making reactive decisions and creating a sense of normality about your situation. Chaos is quite an emotive word to use and, be aware, no matter how talented and prepared you are, there will certainly be a personal sense of chaos at the beginning of your first headship in particular. I could have been signing anything when the business manager left me the documents for signing each day during that first term. I'm not aware that that were any catastrophes as a result, but I certainly wouldn't have had a clue about what to do if there had been! An important question to consider involves asking whether something / someone needs to be repaired or replaced. The Jim Collins analogy about people on the bus in his book, *Good to Great (2001)* is well known. A major act of repair at the start of my headship involved relocating existing staff into situations that they were better suited to. By the start of the new academic year, the Year 2 teacher had migrated to Year 6, an interventions teacher became my EYFS lead, an EAL group teaching assistant became a TA in EYFS and a Year 3 teacher became a Year 1 teacher. Every one of these decisions proved to be successful. I had a significant number of existing capable staff, they had just been in the wrong place.

Repairs can be fairly quickly implemented. Acts of replacement however, depending on the circumstances, can be both more challenging and time consuming. They are a whole other book! In such circumstances, the most important thing as the leader is that you have a vision in place and are ready to act upon it once the opportunity is presented or a process has been completed.

## Fragility

If you are reading this as an experienced leader within your context, that sense of normality described in Carter's model is likely to be well established. Hopefully, by now, you will have made excellent progress in line with your expectations and achieved considerable success. You may, however, as a result of the success of your team, have lost some of your middle or senior leaders to promotion. The reality of school leadership is that stability is fragile, and situations change.

I am reminded of the experience on my shadow inspection prior to becoming a school inspector. The previous inspection report had described the school as "rapidly improving" and had been a highly positive read. In the years since, key staff had left due to promotion and both the head teacher and the deputy head teacher had been on maternity leave, including a concurrent period and had only returned during this particular year. My heart went out to them and I'm glad that I wasn't actually on the inspection team. The reason that I share this story is because you never know when the normality of a situation can be completely changed without you having done anything negative to cause it.

## Future Proofing

Understanding your situation not only requires you to live in the present, it requires you to imagine the future. The story goes that Napoleon was leading his army across France in the scorching heat. When telling his right-hand man, Berthier that he wanted his soldiers *"to march through the avenues of France in the shade"*, Berthier explained that for that to happen, they would need to grow trees and that it would take twenty years. Napoleon responded, *"Exactly – that is why we must start today!"*

I do not wish to stray into the realms of leadership actions in this chapter. The brilliance illustrated in the story above is that an experienced leader should not only be able to quickly gain an accurate assessment of their current situation but should also be looking to create a legacy of their leadership which includes envisaging a situation in the future.

The period when schools were closed during the Coronavirus pandemic demonstrated to various degrees how successfully school leaders were able to gain control out of chaos. In the main though, these were reactive measures. Until this point, the debate around the use of technology and remote learning had centred around whether one had a traditional or progressive view of education. The pandemic moved this debate onto what additional measures needed to be put in place so that this type of teaching and learning could take place. The situation had forced a change of perspective and action in everyone. In the years to come, whilst my personal view is that the humanity of teachers and the importance of relationships will always mean that technology will fall short in some respect, the legacy of this pandemic will be that the education sector will engage in major collaborative work so that when we're faced with another global challenge, we will have a ready to go system which can act as the new normal. Once a situation has been faced once, it can be better faced in the future.

### Things to look for

Stephen Tierney, in his book *Liminal leadership* (2016), helpfully refers to the 5Ds to be investigated within the first 100 days of headship so that you have a good appraisal of the situation you're facing. These are:

Diet – what does the curriculum look like?

Delivery – how good is teaching and learning?

Development – what is the quality of CPD? How broad and deep is it? *(I would add "What is the impact?")*

Democracy – What is the culture?

Demography – what is the student profile? What is on the horizon and what do we need to do in the future?

These Ds by definition, give you an understanding of the behaviour required of you in your first days as leader of a school. You are required to be out and about, seeing everything. You will need to have conversations at all levels with as many people as you can, and you will need to have an eye on the future.

## Problems and Dilemmas

An important distinction to be able to make when assessing your situation comes with an understanding of the difference between problems and dilemmas. Jocelyn Davis in her 2016 book, *The Greats on Leadership* (one of my favourite leadership books), explores this brilliantly. She describes a problem as, *"A challenge with a potential solution; you find and apply the solution and the problem goes away."* A dilemma, however, has positive and negative sides, neither of which can stand alone as the correct and permanent answer. Whatever benefit you may achieve in choosing one option, there will have to be some negative consequences as a result. Therefore, your task as a leader is to weigh up the pros and cons before deciding on the best option available at the time. Davis goes on to explain how some of the biggest mistakes are made by people confusing dilemmas with problems and responding inappropriately. This concept is worthy of reflection as a leader of a school. We often find ourselves trying to find the perfect answer to something which we consider to be a problem when, on calm reflection, it's a dilemma. Think of a staffing issue, a budget issue or a personal issue. There's a relief that comes with understanding that, maybe, what you're facing can't be solved, it can only be lived through to the best of your ability.

## Learning Journey

So far, we've reflected upon ourselves and our leadership predispositions and now we've considered how we face a new situation and our approach to the people and the other elements involved. We've also seen how situations can change and that it's important to understand whether what you're faced with is a problem or a dilemma.

Ultimately, the Leadership Matters model invites you consider two important elements about your situation: What is important? What is within your control? Once you know the answer to these two questions, it's time to prepare to do something about it.

These questions may prove helpful:
What strikes you about your current situation?
Who are the key people involved?
Are you focused on the present or the future?
Are you facing a problem or a dilemma?
What is most important now?
What is within your control?
What will you do?

# 3

# Growing Together

*"Turn your face toward the sun and the shadows will fall behind you"*
**Maori Proverb**

The most substantial section of the Leadership Matters model focuses on leadership actions. It takes a step by step journey through David Pendleton's Primary colours model (see below). This chapter will look at the first two stages which involve setting the strategic direction and creating alignment.

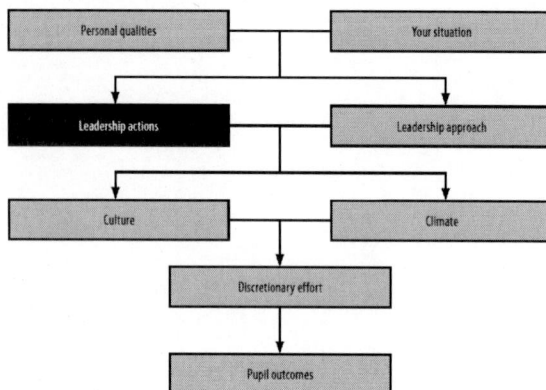

## Foundation of a vision

Bill Gates said, *"Most people overestimate what they can do in one year and underestimate what they can do in ten years."* Vision takes time to become reality. Also, whilst change is inevitable, progress isn't. Setting the strategic direction involves having a long-term view. We've all read of schools that have apparently been transformed at lightning speed. I am not concerned in this book with questioning the success of other individuals or organisations, be it their motivation, methods or outcomes. I do believe though, that for one to be totally fulfilled in a position of school leadership, it is best when one has a genuine passion for the school itself based on its foundation, its values and its history.

One of the things beyond its Christian foundation that attracted to me to St Leonard's was its 200 years of history. It was a real privilege to be head teacher in that bicentennial year. My curiosity in the school's past was at the heart of my vision for its future. I wanted to find out exactly who St Leonard was. He turned out to be the patron saint of prisoners and also women in childbirth – not the easiest of patronages to have associated with your school! However, near the end of this book when we look at how we're inspired by our school history, I'll explain how we are staying true to St Leonard's calling.

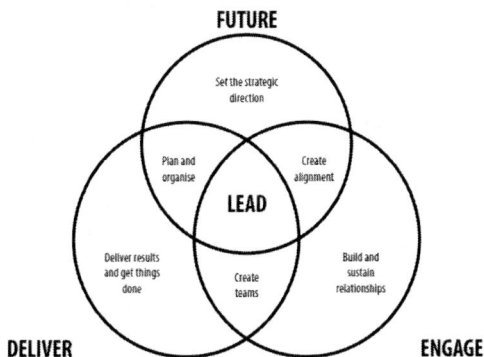

**FUTURE**

Set the strategic direction

Plan and organise

Create alignment

**LEAD**

Deliver results and get things done

Create teams

Build and sustain relationships

**DELIVER**

**ENGAGE**

Andy Buck uses the Pendleton model and cleverly fuses it with Steve Radcliffe's *Future, Engage, Deliver* philosophy from his book, *Leadership Plain and Simple*. Radcliffe tells readers that if there is only one idea about leadership which he wishes them to take from his book, it's that they understand that, *"first and foremost, it's about being in touch with what you care about and then going for it."*

Radcliffe then asks the reader directly, *"What do you care about?"* My original post-it response is still stuck in my copy of the book. It reads as follows:

∞ Outcomes / values for children
∞ Arts education
∞ Influence on individuals and wider profession
∞ Legacy

Whilst I could have placed these factors in the first chapter of this book, what one stands for is also at the foundation of setting a strategic direction. Whilst it's informed by the past, it is focused on the future. Looking back on this post-it note I can clearly see the progression in my headship journey – where it had come from and where it was heading. As the leader of an organisation, it is vital that you can transfer this motivation from being personal to being collaborative at the earliest opportunity. This involves sharing and establishing clear values which permeate through every aspect of school life.

## Values

The choice of illustration for the cover of this book is not coincidental. The lighthouse is firmly founded in the rock. Without the rock, there is no sustainable light to be shone. The lighthouse on the rock in this instance is not synonymous with a person or a role but with the values of the school.

Naturally, you will understand that as a Church of England primary school, one could describe St Leonard's as being rooted in Christian values. It is also a school which is situated in a hugely diverse community within London. St Leonard's is a Christian school; it is not a school for Christians. In the same way that I wish this book to be inclusive, I felt it vital that, under my care, the values I wished to have underpinning the new strategic direction of the school were both explicitly Christian and accessible to all. As such, I chose the following Bible verses to share with staff on day one of my headship: *"But the fruit of the Spirit is love, joy, peace, patience, kindness, goodness, gentleness, faithfulness and self-control. Against such, there is no law." (Galatians 5: 22-23)*

I'll consider the choice of these verses from a Christian perspective within the epilogue. For now, though, I hope that you can see that these values are something which anyone would wish to show toward each other and to nurture in children irrespective of different backgrounds. These values are always shared with parents on tours and I've yet to meet anyone who's not been able to comfortably identify with these criteria. Similarly, when we are in discussion with a child following an incident of undesired behaviour, the fruit of the spirit are always the starting point. The three school rules we have (play safely and sensibly; keep your hands, feet and unkind comments to yourself; do as an adult tells you the first time) are only used to supplement the discussion. Being disappointed that someone hasn't lived up to our values is more powerful and chastening than telling someone they've broken the rules.

Before one can expect these values to be understood and adopted by the children, they need to be modelled as behaviours by the staff, starting with oneself. As humans, the behaviours we find most difficult to model will differ according to the individual. Patience is not abundant within my personal fruit vine. I don't know where I was when patience was being given out, but I somehow missed out – I probably was in too much of a rush to wait for it!

When I joined St Leonard's, there was an ulterior motive behind my selection of the fruit of the spirit as the chosen set of values. I'd been made aware by the Chair of Governors that there had been issues surrounding certain staff relationships going on for a significant period of time. As such, on day one, I challenged all staff to consider how we were to expect to see the fruit of the spirit in our children if we couldn't show it towards each other.

## Forgiveness

In understanding the importance of values, it is also important that one accepts the imperfection of our humanity. It is very rare in a school that one sees an adult who has gone out of their way to deliberately upset another individual. The ability to accept people for who they are and to keep one's eye on the bigger picture is a crucial part of keeping the organisation aligned to the vision and the values you've brought to the school. Forgiveness is crucial if a school community is to remain unified. It's best to have the mind-set that there are very few acts which are unforgiveable. Similarly, those who have fallen short of the school's values need to accept that, amongst other possible consequences, this undermines trust (something we'll look at when we discuss the importance of teams). Forgiveness can be easier to talk about than to practise. It may need to be seen differently in an organisational context when compared with an individual one, as it cannot be limitless within a school. Individual errors are one thing; disloyalty and the systematic undermining of others is unacceptable and must be challenged and dealt with. As a leader, one does have to be prepared to enforce the ultimate sanction for the greater good. The undermining of the school's values is inextricably linked with the undermining of your leadership.

### Formation of Strategy

Aligned to your vision and values, a strategy is more than an approach or a plan. It is a process which should involve consultation, reflection and the application of knowledge based on experience. As the leader, the responsibility lies with you to begin and energise this process.

Goals → Current Position → Opportunities → Risks → Next Steps

(based on Greenway, Blacknell, Coombe - 2018)

Goals need to be set. There needs to be a clear rationale behind why you are setting a particular goal as well as having a clear set of criteria demonstrating what success will look like.

There needs to be a shared understanding at all levels of the current position. We'll explore this more when we discuss creating alignment, but this process involves governors, senior leaders, middle leaders and ultimately the whole staff team in some capacity. A key question to ask at this point is, *"Where are we on our journey?"*

Seeking out opportunities is an absolutely vital part of the process. Having the courage to ask for help from beyond your own setting as well as looking for talent development within your own team will bring great benefit. I'll give some specific examples later in the book when we look at delivery and results, but an essential part of our school's success in its journey from good to excellent was based on our strategy of sourcing expertise from elsewhere when we didn't have it within our own school. The teaching profession is full of people willing to support each other. I've never had a request for help made to my colleagues turned down. It's absolutely the case, that our school improvement journey was accelerated because part of our strategy included asking for help.

Risk management is also an important part of strategy formation. As someone who likes to focus on the big picture, whilst it's not the case that I'm blind to risk – it's just that it doesn't stop me. This is a great example of why the strategy needs to be developed in a consultative way. There will be others on your team who are fine detail type people. They're easy to spot – they usually walk around with fancy notebooks and their life is a series of lists!

I'm not knocking these fine individuals. They are absolutely crucial in keeping us big picture impresarios grounded. They are also instrumental in ensuring that what starts as a big idea in an office successfully gets implemented in an organised way within the classrooms. This links beautifully with the *Zone of Growth* concept described in the Leadership Matters model.

Adapted from Yerkes and Dodson (1908), the model below looks at the correlation between the level of challenge and the level of growth. The sweet spot to aim for is what they refer to as *the zone of stretch*. If your strategy is appropriately considered, the staff should be brought out of their comfort zone but not taken near the zone of panic.

The time to use this model is at the planning stage. It's too late if it's an observation being made at the implementation stage. The damage will have already been done.

Development

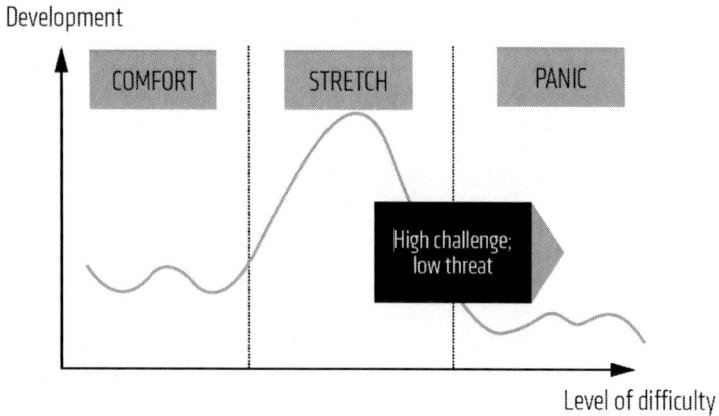

Level of difficulty

Therefore, the "next steps" part of the process involves looking at the mid-term priorities. Whilst it's important to keep your eye on the final goal, having mini goals to achieve along the way not only break down the process into clearly visible and manageable steps, they also give everybody a chance to experience success along the way. Your team feeling successful is an important aspiration to have within your overall strategy.

**The STOP Model**

In *Leadership Matters,* Andy Buck shares this very simple model which you may wish to use with the aim of making good decisions:

*Situation*
Have you properly understood the situation? What additional information would it be useful to acquire before you make a decision?

*Temptations*
What is the potential to make a biased decision? In particular, how are you making sure you aren't making a decision based on an emotional response?

46

*Options*
What are your options? Take some time to think through other ideas, not just doing the first thing you think of. What else could you do?

*Plan*
This could be as simple as a short to-do list or a more complex plan, depending what is involved.

Using STOP can prevent you from making rash decisions. However, the model doesn't mean you should ignore your intuition. Your instinct can often help you make difficult decisions as part of a carefully considered process. Andy argues that the very best decisions are taken on the basis of, *"a good slug of logic combined with a dash of intuition."*

## Creating Alignment
The creation of alignment is the bridge between setting the strategic direction and the building of sustained relationships within the Leadership Matters model. It's also the point where we move from the future to the engage section of Radcliffe's model.

The most critical element within the creation of alignment is the quality of communication and its clarity. How many times in your own experience has the failure to carry out a task or the resentment shown by a member of staff been attributed to communication? How many times have you been on the receiving end of a poorly communicated plan? You will know just how important communication is. The best school leaders are relentless in the reinforcement of their expectations. They talk about them at every opportunity. They continually show staff that they value and appreciate the contribution an individual may be making.

On a day-to-day basis, when these leaders are walking around school, they are looking for things to praise and comment on, both with pupils and staff. The odd passing comment can mean a great deal to the individuals concerned and they stay motivated as a result. It also underlines to everyone what matters and what is important. This drip-feeding of expectations as part of everyday interactions helps to create and sustain a culture.

Sometimes it is the quiet word to one side that is most effective, particularly if one knows the person doesn't like receiving praise publicly. For others, it is the public thanks at weekly briefing that is most important. Again, this not only motivates the individual concerned but also sends a message to other colleagues about what is important and valued.

## Clarity of Pedagogy

What the most successful schools have done is make sure that every child has a teaching experience that promotes the best possible learning outcomes right across the curriculum, regardless of which teacher they have. They have also managed, by and large, to ensure the job of the teacher is manageable.

To achieve this, schools have often undertaken an internal debate: Should our school have an overall pedagogical framework? At St Leonard's the answer to that question is an emphatic *"yes"*. We teach and learn through the International Primary curriculum (IPC). At the heart of our pedagogical development is our Learning Policy.

This means that all topics contain an established structure in terms of content and assessment. Similarly, we have a standardized approach to teaching calculation and genres of writing. Whilst some would suggest that this could be restrictive for teachers, we have found that it has created a willingness to learn new skills as well as an understanding of where expertise lies within our school. Also, teachers bring their own passion and experience to all of the topics taught. They are not clones, nor are they asked to be. It simply is a case, that it enables children to access new learning more quickly.

## Governors

The process of alignment began the day you were appointed. I remember sharing the presentation of my vision with the governors on my appointment panel. How you communicate your vision when under pressure may ultimately be the difference between being appointed or not. Following that day, you will of course need to keep that channel of communication open with your governing body as they are key strategic partners acting on behalf of children and their families. If you're reading this as a senior leader as opposed to a head teacher, the same principle applies. Whoever appointed you felt that you would fit in with the school's vision and values. Presumably you felt able to align yourself to them, otherwise you shouldn't have joined the school!

At St Leonard's each year, we have a vision evening which all staff and governors attend together. It is a key date in the annual calendar of events because it is the one occasion where we are all focused together as one community on understanding the key priorities in developing the strategic direction of the school. The governors should not be a group of monitors who merely attend meetings to scrutinise data and budget forecasts (though this is an important duty, of course). They need to be included as part of that big picture.

Occasionally, I hear from other head teachers expressing frustration at the behaviour of individual governors or collective governing bodies. This usually comes down to an instance where someone is perceived to be straying from the strategic into the operational. One can't expect to avoid ever experiencing such an occasion, but if you clearly plan for opportunities to involve governors in meaningful dialogue with the wider team and if they can see the life of the school in action, there is a greater chance that alignment will be achieved.

The Leadership Matters model refers to the Framework for Governance (National Governors' Association 2015) which is broken down into three stages. Firstly, it states that the setting of School Strategy should ultimately be agreed by the governors and it should be developed in consultation. Hence the reason for our vision evening. The second stage involves governors seeing that the school's development plan does indeed align with the agreed strategy. The final stage involves governors monitoring (but not interfering with) the implementation of practice. The importance of having good communication with governors cannot be overstated, nor can the need to speak with an advisor when there's an ongoing problem.

**Senior Leaders**
We'll look at this more when we discuss the creation of teams. This group of people are absolutely essential not only to the chances of achieving shared success against your goals, but also in terms of securing your own well-being at work. I referred in chapter one to examples of how members of your senior team can intervene on your behalf to avert problems, but they are so much more than that. They are the greatest influencers on strategy. They are the ones whose personality profiles can plug the gaps in your own leadership capacity. They are the encouragers but they should also be the critics. If you haven't got open communication with your senior leadership team you are doomed to fail.

Sometimes you'll hear head teachers say that the job can be "lonely". Whilst on occasions an accountability measure may make one feel very vulnerable, I can honestly say that I've never felt lonely in the role. We'll look at relationships in the next chapter.

On the rare occasion that there's been the need for a decision to be made and it's clear that it's only going to be based on a majority rather than a unanimous decision, I ask senior leaders to identify as one of the following types:

- ∞ Wholeheartedly endorse and support
- ∞ Have minor reservations but able to actively support
- ∞ Have lots of reservations but prepared to support
- ∞ Unable to support

By doing this, everyone has a clear idea about everyone's position at the meeting itself which, in turn is likely to minimise the probability of any subsequent unhelpful private discussion. As a leader though, you do need to be aware of any introverts in the team. They may find vocalising their thoughts more uncomfortable. As such, it's important that they are aware of the process before such circumstances ever arise. Please also note that *unable to support* does not mean *actively undermine*. Such occasions are definitely ones where confidentiality is paramount.

## Middle Leaders

Andy Buck describes these leaders as the engine room of a school which is a great analogy. If your middle leaders are not on board, your vision at best is going to be very slow in being realised, and at worst is going to be derailed. We'll look more at this group in chapter 5 when we focus on delivery and results. High quality appraisal supported by excellent professional development opportunities is key to creating alignment with this team. The vast majority of leaders genuinely wish to do an excellent job. They also need to feel that their career is progressing somewhere, that they are learning the skills and gaining the knowledge and experience necessary to become senior leaders.

Currently, I'm a trainer for the NPQML for the schools within the SDBEMAT. Overwhelmingly, the biggest factor declared by participants which affects whether they feel aligned to the improvement process within their school or not is time. As a school leader, you must find time for these teachers to engage in the strategic process of improving teaching and learning in their subject. They want to become leaders not merely managers. As a school leader, a return on your investment in the development of middle leaders will be realised as they become your senior leaders of tomorrow. One of the most satisfying aspects of headship is seeing such professionals progress under your guidance and support.

## What alignment looks like

You'll know that you've created alignment when you can see not only a sense of purpose at all levels within your community, but you'll see the evidence of personal and collective trust beginning to emerge. You'll feel confident that not only can everyone articulate the school's goals and priorities, but that they can also articulate their place in the grand scheme of things. It's at this point that you can really begin to harvest the fruit of your vision and strategy by focusing on deepening professional relationships and by creating teams.

Key questions which may prove helpful to support your reflections on this chapter are:

How do you clearly communicate your vision to different stakeholders?

What are the fundamental values which drive your leadership?

What is the ultimate goal that you're working towards?

What is the current position?

How do you engage with different stakeholders in the development of a strategy?

How do you create alignment within your teams?

# 4

# Amazing Grace

*"Better to illuminate than to merely shine."*
**Thomas Aquinas**

Two vital aspects of the Leadership Matters model include "Build and sustain relationships" and "Create teams". Central to the model is the creation of what Andy Buck refers to as culture and climate. Culture is described as *"the way we do things here"*, whilst climate refers to how it *feels* to work in a particular organisation. These two elements combine to create what is described as *"discretionary effort"*. The amount of discretionary effort realised depends on how successfully as a leader you've created a situation where people are prepared to go the extra mile for the cause.

**Grace**

Each year, the Southwark Diocesan Board Head Teachers' Association holds its conference within the spectacular grounds of Canterbury cathedral. It's a conference which draws its audience from a wider body than merely head teachers. Deputy and Assistant head teachers are also welcome, as are members of the clergy who have schools in their parish. In 2019, The Venerable Chris Skilton challenged those present to reflect on the following question: *"What have you not had to work for that has instead been given to you as an act of grace?"*

Again, I will leave the Christian context involved to the epilogue of this book. Reflecting silently on the question, all I could immediately come up with was "the new building". So in typical Simon style, I changed the question! However, I only changed one word. I replaced *"what?"* with *"who?"*. Now my pen was able to go into overdrive. It was certainly the case, after being at St Leonard's for some years, that I could see the staff team as a gift. For their incredible talent and commitment to be seen by me as anything different, would be to take credit for success where it is not due.

Sir Ken Robinson in his book, Finding Your Element (2013) considers the vocational dimension of our lives through the analogy of a voyage. He states that, whilst charting your course, *"you meet new people and have new experiences; you influence them and they affect you and together you change the stories of one another's lives."*

## Relationships

Read the above quote again. If ever a couple of lines summed up the importance of relationships in both our individual lives as well as in the development of a team, surely it is those words. What Robinson understands is that, whilst there will be some people who walk into your school, there will be others who walk into your life as they do so. It is for this reason, that work has the ability to profoundly affect our own sense of well-being. Whatever joys or frustrations are caused by the tasks involved in our work these are nothing compared with those feelings experienced as a result of the quality of our relationships at work.

Think of someone with whom you have a naturally positive rapport. Irrespective of any difficulty contained within the topic of conversation, it's simply a joy to be in their company. Now think of a relationship which you have to work harder at. Whatever feelings arise, they must not prevent you from having positive dialogue for the sake of the wider culture and climate.

In your role, you will experience all sorts of relationships. Some you will manage more easily than others. However, it is important to have in the back of your mind, Peter Drucker's quote (referred to in the Leadership Matters book), *"Culture eats strategy for breakfast."* If you are unwilling or unable to invest in the building of relationships, all that you've reflected on in the previous chapters will count for very little.

## Personal or Professional

If you are reading this chapter without having either completed LM Persona as referred to in chapter one or LM360$^0$ (which we'll look at in this chapter) then it may be worth reading it again in isolation once you have completed these assessments. This is because the quality of your professional relationships is entirely dependent upon your ability to be both self-aware as well as your ability to offer and receive feedback to and from others.

If you do not have access to the Leadership Matters materials, then simply take the time to reflect on your personality once again but also, this time, consider asking for feedback from other people within the different sectors of your organisation.
In my case, I'm acutely aware of how my own predispositions may affect the foundation of my relationships.

First impressions really do count with me. In personal relationships, how that first experience unfolds will usually decide whether the door is left permanently open or permanently closed, bolted, reinforced, alarmed and fitted with CCTV. However, in professional relationships, one has a duty to keep the door open at least slightly (and often with the help of someone else holding it open on your behalf). Everyone needs to be able to pass through somehow. One has to *"leave a light on."*

As a school leader, you have to be able to look yourself in the mirror when a professional relationship has been damaged and be able to honestly assess that it was the other person who turned out the light, either by their behaviour or their incapability. All of this being said, it's important that we always remember in schools that the children come first.

Relationships are complex. Cherish the ones you enjoy. Learn from the ones which challenge you. Most of all, when engaging with someone else, be clear in your own mind whether the exchange is personal or professional.

## Friends or Allies; Foes or Adversaries

In her book, *The Greats on Leadership* (2016), Jocelyn Davis brilliantly explains the nuanced differences involved between personal and professional relationships.

Friends are unconditionally for you in the same way as foes are unconditionally against you. Whilst not impossible (through the power of forgiveness), it is unlikely that someone will transfer from being a foe to being a friend. However, whether someone is an ally or an adversary depends upon the issues involved and the perceived impact upon them or their protected interest. The line between ally and adversary is permeable.

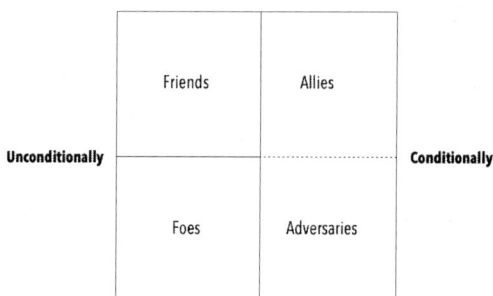

|  | Friends | Allies |  |
|---|---|---|---|
| **Unconditionally** | | | **Conditionally** |
|  | Foes | Adversaries |  |

Davis argues that some of the biggest errors made by leaders arise when they have misunderstood the foundation of their relationship or its purpose. I have seen this error made in schools several times over the years. Whether it's the leader who won't do the right thing for the children or the staff because of their relationship with a poorly performing teacher or governor, or whether it's someone who's taken a professional decision personally from a position of friendship, the consequences can be deeply undesirable.

It has to be said that I approach decision making in professional relationships very differently from how I do with personal ones. Professionally, I very much rely on logic, whereas personally, I'm far more prone to being emotionally persuaded. As a school leader, this links with what I mentioned in the earlier chapter about not feeling lonely in headship but sometimes feeling vulnerable. The reason I'm not lonely is because I am focused on making alliances rather than friends. That is not to say that a school leader should be unfriendly or that friendships do not result from an alliance. However, whereas when one joins a school as a class teacher, it is important to make friends as well as cooperate with colleagues because a positive social life can bring about great benefits, as a head teacher you have to be seen by the wider community to be keeping the focus on the wider professional outcomes. It is possible as a school leader to have friends at work but choose them very carefully. Ultimately whether you treat someone as a friend, ally, adversary or foe will depend upon the level of trust as well as the level of ability involved.

## Building trust

Collaboration and partnership are words commonly preached in the world of education. Whilst these characteristics are vital, all too often people expect this to happen without really taking time to consider the conditions that allow for such effective practice to take place or what it actually looks like on the ground. The Leadership Matters approach adapts the Steven Covey model from his book *The Speed of Trust* (2008).

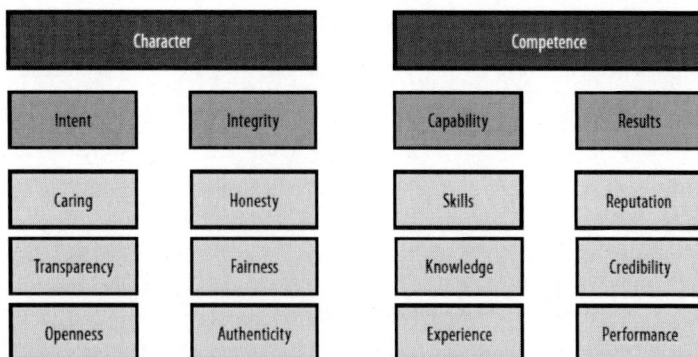

| Character | | Competence | |
|---|---|---|---|
| Intent | Integrity | Capability | Results |
| Caring | Honesty | Skills | Reputation |
| Transparency | Fairness | Knowledge | Credibility |
| Openness | Authenticity | Experience | Performance |

It is vital to invest time in creating a climate of trust where you are able to concentrate your energies and talents on reaching your goals, rather than spending time engaged in unproductive and misdirected activity associated with concerns about others' motives and unnecessary bureaucracy.

In Covey's view, where levels of trust are low, staff will be working in an unproductive environment which is sometimes associated with unrest and where they are often divided into political camps. It's an environment where bureaucracy slows down productivity and creates low levels of innovation and development. Inevitably, discretionary effort is low.

In teams with a high level of trust, systems and procedures are helpfully aligned and bureaucracy is kept to a minimum. Individuals are trusted and supported to carry out their work. There are positive and transparent relationships among staff, leading to innovation, confidence and loyalty, and discretionary effort is high.

### How do you build trust as a leader?

As Covey helpfully suggests, there are just two key elements to building people's trust in you. The model demonstrates that trust is established based on one's *character* and one's *competence*.

The aspect that really resonates for me in this model is that experience is just one of twelve overall components. When I joined St Leonard's, there was a perception amongst class teachers that career progression within the school was based on a natural order. You waited your turn and you couldn't jump the queue. If I had adopted that approach, we would have most definitely gone backwards.

As a leader, you have to be transparent about what it is that you value when you are looking for leadership qualities in others. You have to have faith in those whom you appoint and be prepared to explain to others why you have that faith in them. This model is a great way of sharing and framing your reasoning. If you appoint well, this will reflect well on you also. Not only will the wider team see the same qualities as you do in the person appointed, but they will develop trust in your decision making.

Another element I love about this model is that it complements Davis' understanding of friends and allies. A person whom you see as being of good character as well as having competence is highly likely to become a friend at some point. If as a leader, you question someone's character, the best that can be achieved is that they become an ally based on their competence. This I believe is an acceptable outcome. You cannot be friends with everybody…and you shouldn't try to. You must, however, try to be an ally and a colleague.

My favourite story about the development of trust concerns the tale of Charles Blondin who, in the summer of 1859, walked 160 feet above the falls several times back and forth between Canada and the United States as huge crowds on both sides looked on with shock and awe. Once he crossed in a sack, once on stilts, another time on a bicycle and once he even carried a stove and cooked an omelette! On July 15, Blondin walked backward across the tightrope to Canada and returned pushing a wheelbarrow.

The Blondin story unfolds that it was after pushing a wheelbarrow across while blindfolded that Blondin asked for some audience participation. The crowds had watched and *"Ooooohed"* and *"Aaaaahed!"* He had proven that he could do it; of that, there was no doubt. But now he was asking for a volunteer to get into the wheelbarrow and take a ride across the Falls with him!

It is said that he asked his audience, *"Do you believe I can carry a person across in this wheelbarrow?"* The crowd instantly shouted that they believed he could. It was then that Blondin posed the question - *"Who will get in the wheelbarrow?"* There are various versions of what happened next, including the volunteer being his manager or his mother. The question remains. Who on your team do you have absolute faith in? Who do you know from your team who has absolute faith in you? When you have your answer, don't ever take that trust for granted.

## Loyalty

If there's one thing that people notice in me, it is the value which I place on loyalty. Within a professional context, this unwavering, unquestioning trait arises out of one's perception of another's character and competence and the trust that has been created. Jonathan Haidt in his book, *The Righteous Mind* (2012), explains that, *"morality binds and blinds"*. As such, loyalty in its purest form is rooted in truth and honesty. The fact that blind loyalty can impact upon our judgment underlines the importance of choosing your allies, and indeed your friends, carefully. Loyalty is not a cheap commodity. It is to the professional relationship what love is to the personal. Schools are often vulnerable places for all sorts of reasons. At some point, people's loyalty may be tested. On becoming a school leader, it is only a matter of time before you'll discover who is absolutely standing in your corner. Remember also, that loyalty is required from you. Once you've taken that leap of faith, make sure that the person who can rely on your loyalty knows it. By definition, they deserve it. Irrespective of their role, their age or their experience, build the wider team around them and back them up…always.

## Creating Teams

The Leadership Matters model places this element as the bridge between *engage* and *deliver* in the Radcliffe model and takes its definition of "team" from Katzenbach and Smith (2003):

*"…a small group of people with complementary skills who are committed to a common purpose, performance goals and approach for which they are mutually accountable."*

By looking for complementary skills, you are not only looking at LM Persona for different personal qualities, but also different skill sets. Moreover, you should be looking for opportunities to ensure that your school team reflects your school community. If you have articulated your vision and strategy well in response to an accurate assessment of your current situation, they should be able to commit to a common purpose. Performance goals may be integrated into high quality staff appraisal on the understanding that this not only requires a level of monitoring and challenge, but also support.

The Leadership Matters team development model below is based upon Andy Buck's reflections on the Tuckman model (1965) and the Lencioni model (2002). Notice where trust is created.

It is fanciful to think that on day one, whether in your relationship with governors or staff, that a high level of trust is going to be present. The most one can expect is high levels of hope. This should be enough to get you started.

I've seen people try and accelerate this process on many occasions. I have never seen it successfully fast tracked. Whether it's new members of a governing body, a teaching or support staff team member or membership of a multi academy trust or federation, you have to give it time. That doesn't mean that you can't have your eyes open looking for key allies. *Leadership Matters* adds descriptors for each phase of the model.

*Formation*
Early days; getting to know each other; lots of saying the right thing; not rocking the boat; OK but superficial relationships.

*Adjustment*

Personal views are asserted; people vying for position; lots of assumptions about motives; misunderstanding and bad feeling is not uncommon; difficult time for the leader to manage.

*Trust*

Trust between team members is developing; they are comfortable in exposing their own worries, fears, vulnerabilities and weaknesses; they are honest with one another; people feel valued, supported and respected by others in the team.

*Debate*

Team members trust one another enough to be able to disagree and argue about decisions and issues without it being personal; the focus is doing the right thing, discovering the truth, not winning an argument.

*Buy-in*

There is genuine buy-in and a strong sense of commitment from all team members when key decisions are taken, even if there has been earlier disagreement, because all ideas and views have been properly considered.

*Performance*

Team members, not just the leader, do not hesitate to hold one another to account for their behaviours and adherence to decisions and standards; there is a shared sense of ownership of the whole team's goals; the team are acting as a single unit and performing highly.

It is important to accept that when a new member of staff joins a team, they are going to have an impact upon it. As such, it's really important to take time periodically to reflect on your performance as a team.

## Senior Leaders

The first external appointment I made to the senior leadership team two years into my headship was somebody who oozed every aspect of the Covey model except experience. I consider this appointment to be the school's most significant step in beginning its journey from good to great because everyone within the school community benefited from it. The bar had been raised. Not only did she shine but she illuminated the way for others. Similarly, when appointing our Early Years leader to our senior leadership team, though experienced, she had not been in our school very long at all and wasn't experienced in the new role. As the saying goes: hire character, train skill. When brilliance walks through the door, you have to act. Sandwiched between these appointments were opportunities for people to progress from within the existing staff. There has to be a blend. People need to see opportunities for themselves, but they also need to trust that you will find the necessary expertise from elsewhere if necessary, as with the recent appointment of our deputy head teacher after the previous one had retired after 25 years in the role.

Leadership Matters has another development tool called LM360°. It's a tool which requires the wider school team to give you feedback on your leadership qualities and performance. I do know of schools which have started their Leadership Matters journey with LM360° and you may wish to too. The reason we didn't was because there were new members to the team and I believe that a high level of trust has to be in place so that contributors can be honest and leaders can be reflective within a spirit of mutual support. We have since completed this tool and found it to be most useful. It ensures that there are fewer blind spots to identify in your leadership. It also gives you clear opportunities to reflect on possible development goals for the future.

Senior leaders need to be given authority and autonomy. Whilst this does not make them any less accountable, once the big strategic decision has been made, your job is to get out of their way and to support and manage them in the way they need. We will explore this further in chapter six.

### Appointing middle leaders

St Leonard's today is very different from how it was at the beginning of my headship. The crucial tier that Andy Buck calls the engine room were at best managers. There was no focus on leadership development at all. Since St Leonard's became a school adopting the Leadership Matters approach, now every teacher gets a copy of the Leadership Matters book at the beginning of their second year if they join as an NQT and at the beginning of their employment if they join us as an experienced teacher. We waste no time in sharing our expectations of them. They are not only here to teach well but also to make personal career progress. If you remember, one of my identified motivations was to influence others. This is an example of the long-term vision and a key part of our retention strategy. I want the teachers of St Leonard's today to become the head teachers of tomorrow.

St Leonard's is one of 32 schools (as of April 2020) across the globe that is accredited to teach the International Primary Curriculum (IPC). For over six years, we relied on having one identified IPC leader. Now we have a plethora of middle leaders driving forward standards in their respective subjects. As such, not only is our curriculum benefiting our children, but our middle leaders are learning the required skills to take up senior roles.

Middle leadership is a crucial part of your own whole school leadership to get right if you are going to create a sustainable plan of leadership succession. I should say that, since our school joined the SDBEMAT in 2018, the number of CPD opportunities for all staff has increased immeasurably. Moreover, since our school has been working over a few years with Andy Buck alongside other Church schools in our London borough, we are now at a stage where middle leaders as well as senior leaders receive specific Leadership Matters support, which is fantastic!

## Support staff

In my experience, these are key players in deciding the culture and the climate of the school. On taking up a school leadership role, you may be tempted to concentrate on what's going on in the classrooms. Do not underestimate the importance of developing a positive relationship with the site manager and the business manager in your earliest days. Bearing in mind, your background is likely to lie in teaching and learning, you need to ensure that the level of discretionary effort in these individuals is high…because you will need to rely on their expertise. Similarly, a great support assistant is worth their weight in gold, but one that lacks ability or initiative can have the opposite effect on a teacher than the one intended. The same principles apply. Communicate clearly, challenge, support and hold to account.

## Governors

Governance is an area which varies massively in terms of its effectiveness in the same way that teaching and learning can. I've been in schools where they've just about got the lid off the biscuit tin by 9:30pm and where AOB is the longest item on the agenda. Similarly, I've known of governing bodies which engage in what Kim Scott describes as "ruinous empathy" in her book, *Radical Candor: Be a Kick-Ass Boss Without Losing Your Humanity* (2017). They turn up, smile, nod and sign what needs to be signed. What's required is what Scott describes as "radical candour". It's a partnership.

A head teacher's relationship with the chair of governors is pivotal in both setting the strategic direction, creating alignment and in monitoring, challenging and supporting the school to improve. The chair of governors who appointed me in 2011 left the role almost as soon as I'd been appointed. To clarify, I don't think she left because of my appointment…I hope not at least!

I was fortunate that the incoming chair of governors was a retired head teacher of a secondary Pupil Referral Unit (PRU). I was supported by someone with the organisational experience, albeit not in a primary context. As a new head teacher this was very reassuring. Committees were hour long meetings. Full governing body meetings were an hour and a half. These meetings were well chaired, pacey and purposeful.

In the years leading up to our successful inspection in 2017, the development of the governance team was crucial in illustrating the breadth and depth of leadership within the school. The path is not always well lit. On occasions, it can feel as if there are competing priorities, especially if the content of the training that has been issued by an outside provider does not adequately reflect the context of your school. This is where the importance of the vision evening comes in. It's a great opportunity for governors to be included in the decision-making process of the whole school direction. It is down to you to share the big picture vision for the school. They have a duty to ask you questions about it. They have a duty to monitor and challenge you and, yes...they have a duty to support you and the staff team in achieving it.

Your task can be made so much easier if your leadership is distributed. If governors can see that you delegate and that you have a clear rationale for developing all staff and, crucially, that they can see progress being made, then they will have every reason to have confidence in you. Having an effective governor visits policy will ensure that governors exercise their legitimate right to ask questions without straying into the area of making judgments.

Recently, a new chair has been appointed. With this comes a new set of skills and a new perspective. As such the team development model has begun again. As a school leader, you need to be prepared for changes in governance, recognising that, quite rightly, it's the aspect of school leadership which you'll have the least direct control over.

## Composition of teams

When talking about England's world cup winning rugby union team in 2003, Will Greenwood declared that, *"The magic was in the mix. We had roundheads and cavaliers, old masters and young Turks. With all that difference, you need a whole lot of togetherness."*

If you follow a team in whichever sport, you should be able to identify with this concept. I was fortunate enough to witness Arsenal's invincible season in 2003 / 2004. A mixture of incredible skill and pace built on an underbelly of rock solid "kitchen sink" defending. They could play but they could also compete.

## Team role theory

According to *team roles theory* there are specific different team roles. These roles can vary and be based on personality, expertise, purpose or skill. The type of roles required for a team depend on the specific goals the team wants to achieve. A team that does not have the ideal composition may encounter difficulty. For example, a team consisting of only creative individuals will generate many ideas, but none of them will be implemented. A team consisting of only experts may lose sight of the big picture. A team will perform better if it is aware of the different roles required to reach a specific goal and is able to include those roles within the team.

There are a number of models which you can access via an internet search of *team roles theory*. You could benchmark your team against the model of your choice. You could use it to identify gaps, opportunities and risks. However, it can also help you as a school leader to appreciate the different skills that your other leaders bring to your organisation. You will have something specific to thank them for; not just a completed task, but something unique that they bring to the team. Where do you see yourself in this model? Where do you need to find an ally?

In Stephen Tierney's book, *Liminal leadership* (2016), he asks you to compare yourself with Mr Men or Little Miss! The Mr Men and Little Misses are based on the five traits used by Hay Group:

∞ Be Perfect
∞ Please People
∞ Hurry Up
∞ Try Hard
∞ Be Strong

Tierney says, *"These traits, repeating patterns of behaviour, we often show throughout our lives. They are our greatest strength and worst enemy in leadership situations."* He is right. I believe that our greatest strengths are indeed potentially our greatest weaknesses. That is why you need to create a team in order to be successful. That is why you need to build professional trust throughout the organisation and nurture and reciprocate the personal loyalty and trust of some. Importantly, whilst seeking out and celebrating diversity, you need to create a whole lot of togetherness. If you're able to do this well, you'll be able to meet new people and have new experiences; you will influence them, and they will affect you and together you will change the stories of one another's lives…for the better.

Some questions which you may find helpful:
What / Who has been given to you as an act of grace?
How will you get feedback about your leadership from the wide team?
Who are your allies?
How will you maintain the boundary between friend and ally in a difficult moment?
Who are your adversaries?
How will you promote diversity and keep a whole lot of togetherness?

# 5

# Fortune Favours

*"Coming together is a beginning. Keeping together is progress. Working together is success."*
**Henry Ford**

The final two aspects of the Leadership Actions section of the Leadership Matters model are *Deliver results and get things done* and *Plan and organise* (which ends one cycle and begins the process of looking to the future once again). Unsurprisingly, they are in the *Deliver* section of Steve Radcliffe's *Future, Engage, Deliver* model.

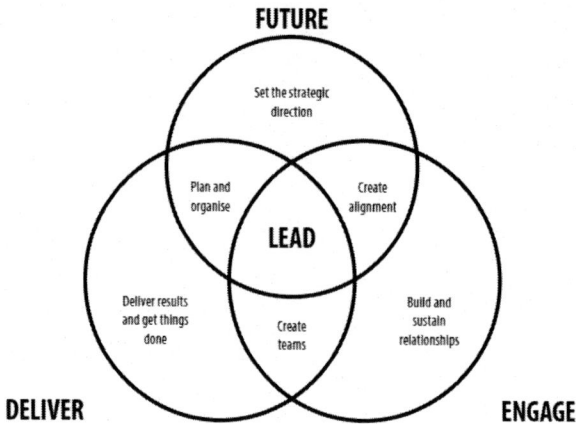

**FUTURE**

Set the strategic direction

Plan and organise

Create alignment

**LEAD**

Deliver results and get things done

Create teams

Build and sustain relationships

**DELIVER**

**ENGAGE**

Radcliffe states, "*Deliver is not a standalone aspect of leading. It follows directly on from Future and Engage.*" This is an important observation to take to heart. It not only exemplifies why action without vision, in line with the famous saying, truly can be a nightmare, but it also underlines the point that it takes time to improve an organisation in a sustainable way and to create momentum which will last beyond your own period of leadership within a school.

In this chapter, I am going to focus on the elements which are particularly pertinent in explaining how the Leadership Matters model has been instrumental in delivering excellence within our school. These are:

∞ Delegation (also relevant to the *Create Teams* section of the Leadership Matters model)
∞ Consistency
∞ Difficult conversations
∞ Prioritisation
∞ Managing change

In all of the above aspects, you need to be bold in your approach. At St Leonard's, we have taken calculated risks and we have had elements of good fortune. But fortune favours the brave.

Andy Buck begins the *deliver results* section of his Leadership Matters book with the following quote from Winston Churchill: *"However beautiful the strategy, you should occasionally look at the results."* In the context of school leadership this takes us directly into the realms of accountability. Whilst the purpose of this book is not to make any argument concerning accountability measures within a national education system, part of its rationale is to underline that for success to be seen to be delivered, it requires scrutiny and a clear trail of responsibility leading all the way to the intended outcome.

## Delegation
There is a very simple framework (Tim Brighouse 2007) that describes nine clear levels of delegation where level one represents no delegation whatsoever and level nine is, in effect, fully distributed leadership.

1. Look into this problem. Give me all the facts. I will decide what to do.
2. Let me know the alternatives available, with the pros and cons of each. I will decide what to select.
3. Let me know the criteria for your recommendation, which alternatives you have identified and which one appears best to you, with any risk identified. I will make the decision.
4. Recommend a course of action for my approval.
5. Let me know what you intend to do. Delay action until I approve.
6. Let me know what you intend to do. Do it unless I say not to.
7. Take action. Let me know what you did. Let me know how it turns out.
8. Take action. Communicate with me only if your action is unsuccessful.
9. Take action. No further communication with me is necessary.

A key tactic within our strategy at St Leonard's was to discover all the expertise available to us, delegate responsibility to the individuals concerned, support and challenge them and, ultimately, hold them to account. We used the Hay Group model (2007) concerning the three key elements needed for delegation as found within the Leadership Matters model.

**Authority**

**Ideal**

**Responsibility**          **Accountability**

As the previous chapter has let you explore your relationships with others and how you will create your teams, we'll assume that the person you're delegating to has the capacity to succeed if the necessary conditions have been created. This involves you as leader taking two important actions.

Firstly, you need to do whatever is necessary to ensure that the whole organisation knows that this person has your authority to lead in the specific area of school development. Failure to do so can result in the leader being undermined. It only takes one person on the team to question this authority for their chances of success to be negatively impacted upon. In my time at St Leonard's, most of the appointments to the senior leadership team have been based on a platform of character and ability rather than specific experience. Overwhelmingly this has proved to be the right strategy for the school. However, it can only work if, as head teacher, one mitigates for any lack of experience by actively promoting the leader's credibility, by showing confidence in their ability and publicly endorsing their authority. A phrase that can regularly be heard within St Leonard's is, *"Allow the leader to lead."*

The second thing that you need to establish as a leader is clear accountability. As the model shows, if there's a lack of accountability, there is too much scope for drift and, let's be honest, you don't drift on target! This being said, in my career I've witnessed head teachers having a misguided understanding of what accountability actually is. Accountability is not the sword of Damocles over someone's head. It is not the hangman's noose. It is not an opportunity to apportion blame. Accountability should be a process which involves reflection at various developmental stages that ultimately forms a judgment against a goal or standard. This process has three elements to it: *monitoring, challenge* and *support.*

Monitoring involves informal conversations as well as formal frameworks such as appraisal. This is why building relationships is so crucial. If your relationship with an individual is right, they are far more likely to come and speak with you about a concern at an early stage. At St Leonard's, we have subject leader forms (see below). These are filled in after a leader has had some dedicated time for their area of leadership. They are not onerous to complete and just give a brief outline of how the time was spent and what the next steps are. Once I receive these, I make a judgment as to whether to stay standing back or whether to invite the leader for a conversation. Crucially, one must acknowledge the content of this dialogue at steady intervals. Showing a regular interest can be enough to encourage the leader to remain motivated.

| Name of Subject Leader | | | |
|---|---|---|---|
| Area of Subject Responsibility | | | |
| Date | | | |
| Focus of Work | | | |
| Classes involved | | | |
| Summary of Activities   (please tick as appropriate) | | | |
| Classroom observation | | Work Scan | |
| Discussion with teacher | | Policy review | |

| Team Teaching | | Discussion with HT | |
|---|---|---|---|
| Demonstrated for Teacher | | Discussion with pupil(s) | |
| Other (please specify) | | | |
| What I have learned as a result of my work | | | |
| Next steps / Aspects I would like clarified / Questions I have | | | |

Challenge is essential if change is to become progress and if progress is to become success. It is one of the key differences between leadership and management. When I started at St Leonard's, it was not unusual to hear, *"We're good. We've always been good and that's all we can be."* I won't explain the rationale behind this opinion as it would divert from the focus of the book. The point is that, as a whole school leader, one of your first priorities is to raise the expectations and aspirations of everyone. A vision evening can be good for this in front of a large audience but it's during those one-to-one conversations with leaders where the inspiration can begin to be realised. It's in these sessions that you can *see the light go on* in their minds. Often a part of challenging a leader involves getting them to challenge others and we'll look at this later on in the chapter.

Support is the aspect which is most often misunderstood or indeed, missing altogether. Accountability is only merited if the person concerned has been supported as well as monitored and challenged. It's not unusual to hear a school leader say something along the line of, *"Well you've had all that time."* Time as we know is a precious commodity, but it's useless if the person concerned does not sufficiently know what they are doing. Support involves dedicated time plus a dedicated resource, be that resource a person or a product. This may be sourced as part of a training programme, by a school partnership or through a relationship with a consultant or improvement partner. The point is, at the beginning of the delegation process, agree the support which needs to be put in place. Set someone up to succeed; then hold them to account.

When success has been achieved, don't forget how important it is to properly credit whoever is responsible. It's important you pass on the credit for success with sincerity, rather than let others think you have been responsible. Nothing is more dispiriting than for a team to see its leader take the credit for something they didn't do!

## Consistency

Andy Buck refers to consistency as being *"A bedrock for creativity and innovation."* This is one reason why I find the Leadership Matters model so appealing. It is rooted in established and accepted leadership theory that ensures that core standards can be met, but it is also designed to encourage leaders to act in a way which can enable their organisations to excel and their stakeholders to flourish. It is an approach, not a scheme.

The school I entered in 2011 was a one form entry primary school. The school now also has a nursery and is expanding to two forms of entry. As such, the challenge of creating consistency has changed for us over time. In the first few years, the staff was a group rather than a team in terms of its approach to teaching and learning. Your experience as a child very much depended on which teacher you were allocated.

Over time, we have worked hard to ensure that, whilst obviously every teacher is uniquely talented with their own personality and natural style, there is a consistent approach to several core elements of teaching and learning. This has been fundamental in improving standards in both the core and foundation curriculum.

A uniformed approach is not something that can be secured overnight. It has taken many years and has involved the work of a great many people. Most importantly, the team understand the need for consistency. They see how in fact it makes what is a very skilled job slightly easier to manage. It helps to create the school's learning culture.

Since having two form entry year groups, there has obviously been an even greater emphasis in this area. Whilst planning and other templates can aid this, the greatest influence on consistency is the relationships between teachers. How we are as a team drives what we do; not the other way around.

One of the biggest challenges faced and achievements made in the past few years involved establishing great consistency whilst under a time pressure. The Early Years leader in post had left St Leonard's in the summer of 2016. She had been instrumental in raising standards in the previous five years. September 2016 saw the opening of a nursery as well as our first two form of entry Reception intake. As such, we had a new Nursery job share team alongside an NQT in one Reception class and an experienced teacher, though new to St Leonard's and to Early Years in the other. Six months later we had our inspection. I'll explain the "how" in our Leadership approach in the next chapter, but the fact that excellence was established and a consistent approach was in place in such a short period of time does demonstrate what can be achieved if everyone can understand the need for action and then commit to doing it.

I remember the SHMI leading the inspection finishing a conversation with me by saying, *"Let's see how far this leadership stretches."* Undoubtedly, this was not just a comment which related to individual talent. It related to teamwork and consistency in all things.

### Difficult conversations
When it comes to tackling under-performance or inappropriate behaviour, there is a continuum, as shown in the diagram opposite.

| Nudge conversations | Direct challenge | Dismissal or agreement |
|---|---|---|
| **Pretty EASY** | **HARDEST** | **Quite EASY** |

If one accepts the need for distributed leadership, teamwork, accountability and consistency, it is inevitable that there are going to be occasions when one has to have difficult conversations or support those whom you've delegated responsibility to in having them.

The hardest conversations to have, the ones we tend to put off more than any others, are those that sit in the middle. You have tried nudging and it hasn't worked. The situation doesn't require dismissal…yet.

One must consider a few factors before embarking on a difficult conversation. Most importantly, you need to be clear about the desired outcome; what is the best-case scenario or the least you are prepared to settle for?

Secondly, you need to consider if you are indeed the best person to be having the conversation. In accepting that the most difficult conversations in the most serious of circumstances must not be delegated, there are often many phases leading up to such a point when choosing a different leader to have the conversation can make the difference between a situation improving or deteriorating. This all goes back to knowing yourself and knowing others. I will regularly sound out the opinion of those I trust completely before attempting to have a difficult conversation. It is during these moments that these fantastic, loyal people are able to navigate between being an ally or a friend as required.

Thirdly, you need to be prepared to see a process to the conclusion that is right for the children and the wider team. In my case, whilst I need to be aware not to be too blunt with people, this does not mean compromising on standards and expectations. If someone isn't up to the job, then they either have to commit to improve or leave.

There are occasions when a leader whom you've delegated something to will come and disclose an issue they're experiencing with another member of staff. Depending on their experience and their character, you may decide to delegate the difficult conversation to them. It's important that your judgment is sound when doing this. If you're right, then as a result of the leader carrying out the task, their authority and credibility will be enhanced. Should you get it wrong, then this could leave them undermined or exposed.

The Leadership Matters model includes a memorable mnemonic, NEFI ART, to assist you in such conversations. This formula needs to be internalised and then you need to practise it repeatedly to become more confident, but there are many occasions when it has proved to be a helpful scaffold. The work of Susan Scott (2003) who is well known for her work in this area, recommends covering the following in that start to the conversation, uninterrupted:

**N**ame the issue
Describe a specific **E**xample
Describe your **F**eelings about the issue
Clarify what is at stake, why this is **I**mportant
**A**ccept your contribution to this problem
Indicate your wish to **R**esolve the issue
Invite **T**hem to respond

I sometimes substitute the *Accept* (the part you've played) for *Acknowledge* (the challenge involved). Critical in the process is making sure that once the situation has been set out you do not go on to try to solve the issue until you have an acceptance from the other person of the validity of the concern.

This all sounds fine in theory, but you need to ensure that you are properly prepared not only to give this introduction, but also for what may follow. There might be a whole range of responses from silence to anger, from complete denial to emotional collapse. Thinking through in advance how you might respond to each of these can be helpful.

You also need to try not to fall into the trap of 'propping up' the discussion that follows. Use questions to get the other person to talk and reflect on the issue, gain understanding and give a commitment to action. Let silences happen rather than be tempted to fill them. As Susan Scott suggests, let the silence do the heavy lifting. If the discussion goes off track, bring the dialogue back onto the issue you raised at the start.

Ultimately though, these difficult conversations can prove to make or break your chances of delivering on your objectives and getting the required results – so you can't avoid having them. Just remember that you're trying to elicit light out of potential darkness. At the very least, your own path needs to be illuminated following the conversation.

## After a difficult conversation
After a difficult conversation it can be tempting to pretend it didn't happen, particularly if the person works closely with you. It can sometimes just be a bit awkward. The best thing is to be proactive and take steps to keep dialogue open. Thank them for the conversation and focus on the agreed outcomes positively. Don't forget to make sure you hold them to account for what they have agreed to. Finally, you may wish to get involved in an activity with the person concerned that is nothing to do with what you have been discussing. Something you both enjoy. In a way, this approach isn't dissimilar from the repair and rebuild we might seek to undertake with a pupil!

## Prioritisation

One of my biggest roles at St Leonard's has been to ensure that we spend as much of our time doing things that are important but not urgent. This involves reflecting on everything which comes your way and asking if it's going to help the mission or hinder it.

Undoubtedly, this has been a significant area of new learning for me since I took up headship. If you remember from my LM Persona report, I'm a "big picture" person. I look at a situation and I look for possibilities. It doesn't matter whether it's an environmental challenge or a curriculum development, I quickly have an idea about how I want it to look. The Director of Education at the Diocesan Board once described me as *"relentless"* during a conversation when he was comparing the situation at St Leonard's with one elsewhere. I don't know if he meant it as a compliment (and I didn't ask!) but I knew that he understood that, at St Leonard's, we wanted to keep momentum with us.

The Leadership Matters model for prioritisation based on the Eisenhower Matrix resonates well with me.

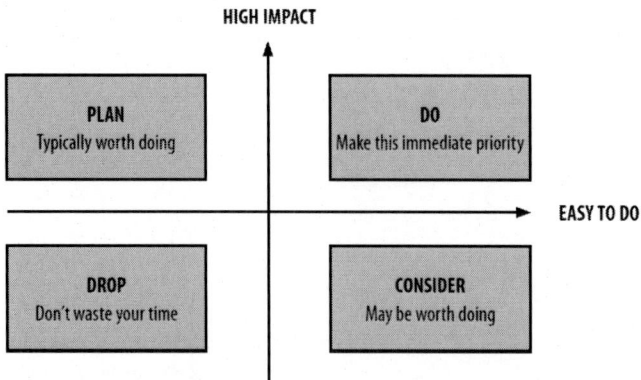

HIGH IMPACT

| PLAN | DO |
|---|---|
| Typically worth doing | Make this immediate priority |

EASY TO DO

| DROP | CONSIDER |
|---|---|
| Don't waste your time | May be worth doing |

What attracts me to this model is that it can be applied to big picture opportunities as well as to the fine details. It is also a great mechanism for keeping things in perspective. I often share with colleagues my thoughts on the difference between pressure and stress. Pressure is both positive and necessary if we are to bring out the best within ourselves and from each other. If you can't handle pressure, then you shouldn't be in teaching and you certainly shouldn't be leading a school.

Stress, however, is altogether different. I have seen good colleagues succumb to stress over the years. In headship, I still see some who try to do everything themselves. Sometimes it's down to their reluctance to delegate and their lack of trust in others. However, on other occasions it's due to the fact that they allow themselves to be buffeted by the storms of the system, be they stemming from the Local Authority or by government. I never cease to be amazed at just how much sent from those two mailboxes belongs in the bottom left quadrant. Ladies and gentlemen, that's what the *Delete* button is for!

As a head teacher, you will be offered opportunity after opportunity to try this or that. Words like "fun" and "engaging" will be attached to all sorts of initiatives. Then of course there's the misuse of the "Ofsted like" and "Research says" terminology. One of the key reasons behind our success is that we have not allowed ourselves to be deflected from our core purpose. We do not take up every opportunity. We do not respond to the latest rumour. We do not seek the approval of others. It's amazing just how much recognition a school can get when it actually doesn't go out of its way to seek it.

Where this model provided me with a steep learning curve in my early days of headship related to the breaking down of initiatives into smaller pieces. What I had to learn was that, whilst some steps were not in any way important for me, they were of the utmost importance to others. As such of course, they were important to me but I just didn't know it! Therefore, if like me you're a big picture thinker, make sure that you consult with the fine detail department to ensure that you are all working in alliance and that they can see the light. Similarly, if you're a step by step thinker, make sure that you are still able to articulate a picture of what it will look like in the end. Otherwise, there'll be some who will lose both faith and interest because all they can see is the tunnel rather than the light.

Once you've identified your priorities for development, you're tasked with leading the management of the change process. *Leadership Matters* is the perfect companion!

### Managing Change

Consider trying this activity the next time you're trying to communicate the need for change to your staff and governor team. It may be a good way to start your vision evening.

Ask everyone to find a partner (the odd triangular trio is also fine). Give them 20 seconds to face each other and notice everything about their appearance. Then tell them to stand back to back. Finally issue the following instruction using exactly these words: *"Change something about your appearance."*

On facing one another, the challenge is for the participants to notice the change which has been made. Give them a short while to work the change out before asking the group how many of them changed their appearance by removing something (Jewellery and accessories such as hair clips, scarves or ties are often removed). I am confident that a number of hands will go up.

The point is this: many people associate change with loss. You hadn't asked people to remove an item. You had simply asked them to change their appearance. But for some, change is synonymous with feelings of loss and grief.

When you think of it, this is quite a profound revelation. For some, change is exciting. People can see the light at the end of the tunnel. For others, though, all they can see is the darkness which surrounds them at the prospect of having to change. If ever the title of this book was appropriate for one aspect of leadership, it's with the leadership and management of change.

All of us, when there is a major change happening, tend to go through a series of stages of how we feel about the change. This can also affect our own feelings of self-worth or competence. It is not uncommon for people to doubt they can perform successfully in the way a change may demand. The most commonly known model for illustrating how this happens was developed by Elisabeth Kübler-Ross (1969).

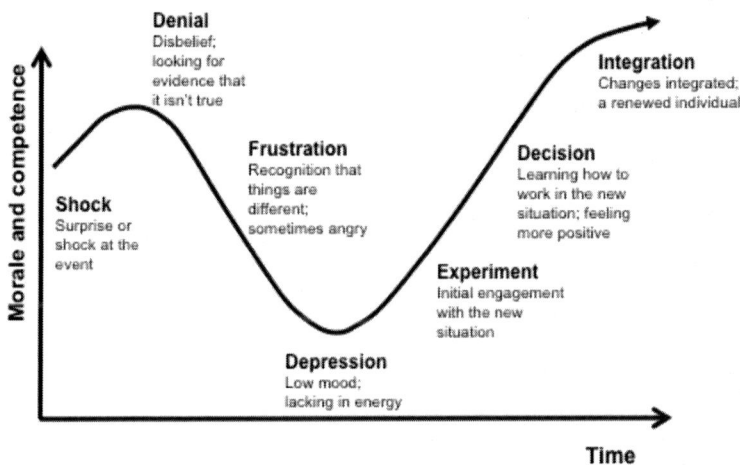

When you are introducing a significant change, it is well worth taking some time out to think about how each of the individuals in the team are likely to react and then work out the best way to approach things with them, without compromising on your overall goals.

The Leadership Matters book contains some great advice on how to manage change, so let's recap on the main aspects covered, beginning with leadership and change management guru John Kotter. A professor at Harvard Business School and world-renowned change expert, Kotter introduced his eight-step change process in his book *Leading Change* in 1996.

*Step one: increase urgency*
For change to happen, it helps if the whole team or the school really wants it. It is about you instigating an open, honest and convincing dialogue about what's happening in the educational landscape and with your context.

*Step two: build a 'change-team'*
In a primary school, this will usually be the SLT but does not need to be exclusively so. Having them as a small group of advocates for the rest of the team can be very powerful, particularly if you have managed to include one or two key influencers in your group.

*Step three: get the vision right*
You need to link these concepts to an overall vision that people can grasp easily and remember.

*Step four: communication for buy-in*
What you and your change-team do with your plans after they have been created is crucial. You need to provide clarity and you need to keep telling the story. It's also important for you, as the driver of the change to 'walk the talk'. What you actually do is often far more important – and believable – than what you say. You should demonstrate the kind of behaviour that you want from others.

*Step five: enable action*
If you follow these steps and reach this point in the change process, you've been talking about the vision and building buy-in. Hopefully, staff want to get busy and achieve the benefits that you have been promoting. At a more senior level, using sub-teams to deliver on a change can be a great way of playing to strengths and keeping things manageable.

*Step six: create short-term wins*
Nothing motivates more than success. Look out for ways you can give your staff a taste of victory early in the change process. People need to quickly be thinking that the change is a good thing – they need to 'feel the benefit' fast.

*Step seven: don't let up*
Kotter argues that many change projects fail because victory is declared too early. Real change takes time to embed.

*Step eight: make it stick*
Finally, to make any change stick, it should become part of your culture. It should be consistently applied. A team's culture often determines what gets done, so the values

behind the vision must show in day-to-day work. Your systems for monitoring need to place a value on the things you have changed to help embed them. The key milestones should be part of the school's development plan. We also link such changes to individual's appraisals.

## Enabling action

Stage five of Kotter's model is about making sure there is nothing to stop a change being successful. This is where the approach which I have used the most at St Leonard's has been most useful. Created by Knoster, Thousand and Villa (2000), the model below has proved to be an essential part of supporting our change management process. It can be used to support discussions in appraisal. It can be used to help structure a discussion when challenging individual performance. Where I use it most often is in discussions with middle leaders, and especially with those new to a role. Andy Buck talks about having a pre-mortem instead of a post-mortem. By engaging in a conversation around this model, one can begin to predict some of the potential obstacles which may appear. One can delay implementing the change if necessary, so as to plug the required gaps. This model can be the difference between setting someone up to succeed or setting them up to fail. One can also begin to think about how to approach members of staff differently in order for them to be able to enact the change successfully.

| Vision | Skills | Incentives | Resources | Action Plans | Success |
|--------|--------|------------|-----------|--------------|---------|
|        | Skills | Incentives | Resources | Action Plans | Confusion |
| Vision |        | Incentives | Resources | Action Plans | Anxiety |
| Vision | Skills |            | Resources | Action Plans | Slow Change |
| Vision | Skills | Incentives |           | Action Plans | Frustration |
| Vision | Skills | Incentives | Resources |              | False Starts |

## The difference between equality and equity

As a whole school leader, you are in the results business. Your challenge is to find a way for everyone to reach the required destination and achieve the desired goal. This means different approaches and different amounts of support for different people. The key to this is ensuring that everyone is investing the same amount of commitment. If people see that everyone is trying their best, they will make a degree of allowance for those who need additional consideration. However, if people see that someone is letting the team down and doesn't seem to be that bothered about it, that's when disharmony in the ranks can appear.

Understanding the difference between equality and equity is central to becoming able to create a culture and climate of success. As a society, we are rightly becoming more aware of issues surrounding equality of opportunity…and we still have a long way to go within the realms of school leadership. However, the word "equality" is based on mathematics. Equity is based on fairness. The image below illustrates this beautifully.

Of course, staffroom politics isn't quite as simple as that and Jonathan Haidt explores the human understanding of fairness brilliantly in his book, *The Righteous Mind* (2012). Ultimately, the vast majority of us have a desire to establish this. For some of us, the concept of fairness is linked to our understanding of what constitutes as an equal share. However, for others, fairness is linked to a condition of proportionality based on one's effort or investment. Depending upon your view of fairness, your relationships with others may be enhanced or compromised. Therefore, as a leader, you've not only got to consider the support required for each individual or group but you've also got to consider how to explain your rationale for these differing levels of support, otherwise you could be open to accusations of positive or negative bias.

If there's one thing that all leaders should understand about managing change, it is that *the message is never what you've said; it's what's been heard.*

Once the launch phase is over, it is important that you continue to monitor, challenge and support your colleagues. There may be misunderstandings which you need to respond to. There will certainly be effort and success which you'll need to acknowledge. The important thing is to try and secure some quick wins so that your initiative gains momentum. If you are a head teacher, remember that you are now primarily an enabler. You are the coach on the touchline, not the dynamic midfielder in the middle of the action. You will not have the time or the energy to play that role and there's a good reason for it.

### The Sigmoid Curve

In an interview for the Leadership Matters website, Mary Myatt talks about school leaders needing to have a *"helicopter view"* of the school. There is no way that one can do this from the heart of the action. A school leader's task is to use all of their experience to create the right vision for the circumstance, communicate it clearly, create the teams necessary to implement it and then to monitor its effectiveness. A key skill to develop is the ability to know when to change something which has brought you great success. This is where one needs to be brave.

It's easy to explain a rationale for change if you're not getting the desired results. But, if you're perceived as being successful, there may be a greater chance of encountering resistance. This is where the Sigmoid Curve has been really helpful for our team.

At our last vision evening, for the ice-breaker task, I asked everybody to place where they thought the school was against this curve.

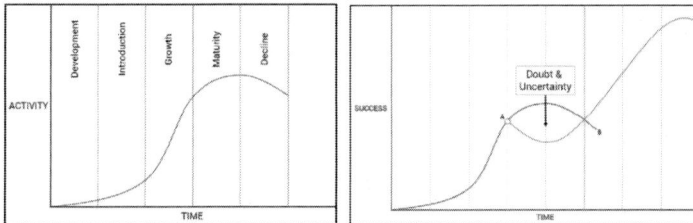

This was a challenging task and it was not without its risk but – fortune favours the brave. Those present included staff who'd been at St Leonard's for varying lengths of time (including a new deputy head teacher) and governors of varying experience (including a newly elected parent governor and a Chair of Governors a term into his role). As such, it was only to be expected that people would have different frames of reference. The key to success though lay in the table discussions where those with the most insight had the opportunity to persuade the other members of their table. I remained an observer.

We came to the conclusion (quite rightly), that whilst the curve would be different for individuals considering their career journey, as a school, we were within the maturity bandwidth. I was really glad that there was a shared understanding of our situation. Had there not been, it would have made our necessary journey so much harder to make. The previous term had been dominated by individual rather than whole school circumstances. As such, it was great to have renewed energy focused on the entire organisation once again.

The thing I love about the Sigmoid curve is that it is simply the natural appliance of human science. There is nothing that can be done to prevent the decline of an original idea. What was happening in our school was entirely natural. The solution lies in being able to pick the right moment to begin to prepare for a new phase of change and growth. As a team of staff and governors, we were not despondent in any way; quite the reverse. I was heartened by the work of the truly professional and committed team of staff I had the fortune to lead. They had recognised what I already knew.

If there's a word I loathe in education, it's *consolidation*. Schools are either improving or declining. They are never holding still. Sometimes they are changing rapidly; sometimes slowly – but they are always changing. To my mind, consolidation provides an excuse to take your eye off the ball. To do so, would be to undo all the good work that you may have done.

St Leonard's is not a place that is afraid of change, and as a leader, nor can you be.

Some questions which you may find useful:
∞ How do you set people up to succeed?
∞ How will you hold them to account?
∞ Do you have the right balance between monitoring, challenging and supporting?
∞ How will you establish consistency?
∞ Where is your organisation on the Sigmoid curve? How do you know?
∞ Where is your career on this curve? What makes you think this?

# 6

# Sailing West

*"Twenty years from now, you will be more disappointed by the things you didn't do than by the things you did do. So, throw off the bowlines, sail away from safe harbour, catch the trade winds in your sails. Explore. Dream. Discover."*
**Mark Twain**

The final section of the Leadership Matters book looks at your leadership approach. It should be said, however, that the model itself is not exactly fixed in terms of the order of its elements. That is just one of the many blessings of the Leadership Matters philosophy. Elements are interdependent when it comes down to charting a course for success.

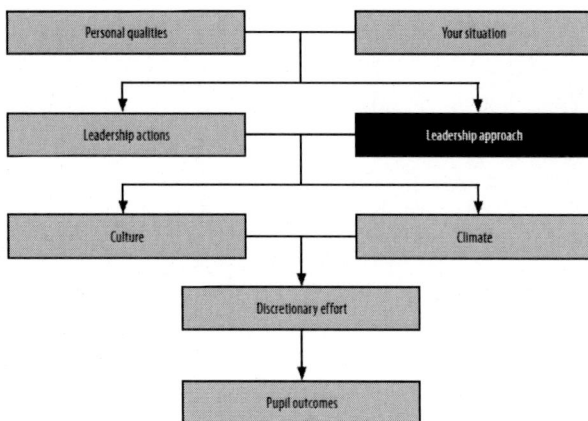

Your leadership approach is focused on *how* you do your job rather than *what* you do. Therefore, it's concerned with your leadership style and how it brings out the best in you and in others.

## Leadership Style required

Let's recap on the leadership style material within *Leadership Matters*. Why does leadership style matter? Are some leadership styles more effective than others? Daniel Goleman, who is probably best known for his work on emotional intelligence, has also investigated the impact of leadership style on the climate of organisations. In his 2000 paper *Leadership that gets results* he identified that, as leaders, we tend to use the following six different leadership styles:

### Visionary (authoritative)
Primary objective: providing long-term direction and vision. You tend to:
∞ develop and articulate a clear vision
∞ solicit staff perspective on the vision and see selling the vision as key to success

∞ persuade staff by explaining the rationale for the team's best long-term interests
∞ set standards and monitor performance in relation to the wider vision
∞ motivate with a balance of positive and negative feedback.

## Affiliative

Primary objective: creating staff harmony. You tend to:

∞ be concerned with promoting friendly interactions
∞ place more emphasis on addressing staff needs than on goals and standards
∞ pay attention to, and care for, the whole person; stress things that keep people happy
∞ avoid performance related confrontations
∞ reward personal characteristics more than job performance.

## Directive (coercive)

Primary objective: compliance. You tend to:

∞ give lots of directives, not direction
∞ expect immediate staff compliance
∞ control tightly
∞ rely on negative, corrective feedback
∞ motivate by imposing sanctions for non-compliance, with few rewards
∞ rarely explains rationale, only negative consequences.

## Democratic

Primary objective: building commitment and generating new ideas. You tend to:

∞ trust that staff can develop the appropriate direction for themselves and the school
∞ invite staff to participate in decisions
∞ reach decisions by consensus
∞ delegate decision-making as well as tasks
∞ hold many meetings and listen to staff concerns
∞ reward adequate performance; rarely give negative feedback.

**Pace-setting**

Primary objective: making rapid progress and achieving tasks to high standards of excellence. You tend to:

∞ lead by example and have high standards: 'look at me; do what I am doing; keep up with me'

∞ expect others to know the rationale behind what is being modelled

∞ are apprehensive about delegating

∞ take responsibility away if high performance is not forthcoming, and have little sympathy for poor performance

∞ rescue the situation or give detailed task instructions when staff experience difficulties.

**Coaching**

Primary objective: long term professional development of others. You tend to:

∞ help staff identify their unique strengths and weaknesses

∞ encourage staff to establish long-range development goals

∞ reach agreement with staff on the team leader's and individuals' roles in the development process

∞ provide on-going advice and feedback

∞ sometimes trade off immediate standards of performance for long-term development.

As you reflect upon the six styles, is there one you tend to predominantly use? Which do you rarely use? Do you make a conscious effort to think about the right approach for any given situation or do you rely on gut instinct?

On the Leadership Matters website, you'll find a diagnostic tool called LM Style which can help you and any of your colleagues better understand your preferred leadership styles and those which maybe are less well developed and could be great areas for personal growth.

Leaders at all levels need to be able to use a range of styles to suit their context and any particular situation.

Daniel Goleman's work also looked at the overall effectiveness of each of the six leadership styles. He identified that the directive and pace-setting leadership styles had a negative impact on climate in the long term, even though there are times when this is absolutely the right approach to take.

This is no surprise in a way. If, as a leader, you find yourself constantly leading by example or telling people what to do because you need to, you are working with people who maybe aren't suited to their roles and need to either improve fast or 'get off the bus'. On the other hand, if are using these styles but don't actually need to, you will be leading a team who feel you don't trust them and probably feel micro-managed.

Goleman also identified that the visionary and affiliative leadership styles were, on average, the most effective overall, closely followed by the democratic and coaching styles.

### Your school's journey
Taking a moment to think about your leadership approach and in particular the right style for your current context or situation, has the potential to make a big difference to the discretionary effort in your staff team. When it comes to thinking about the typical journey of improvement most schools (or teams) go through, Andy Buck has created the illustrative model below.

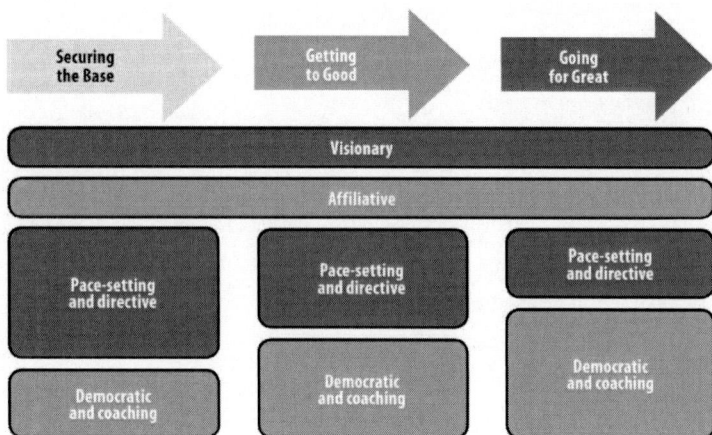

As one can see, whilst communicating the goal and securing positive relationships are vital at any stage of your leadership journey, at the earliest stages, there may be the need to emphasise the importance of high standards and the need for excellence as well as giving a lot of direct instructions. In my case, it also involved confronting unacceptable behaviour from a teacher and inadequate teaching.

Eighteen months into my headship, the two biggest barriers to standards and morale had been removed. This enhanced my personal authority and also energised those remaining to make the required progress for the benefit of the children.

Thereafter, the degree to which you need to be pace-setting and directive ought to decline over time. Conversely, you should be gradually increasing how much you use the democratic and coaching leadership styles. To paraphrase Joel Klein, 'You can mandate adequacy, but you have to unleash greatness'.

The challenge for leaders at all levels is recognising when the context you are working in has improved, and then adapting your style to suit the change. Too often, leaders can get stuck with the leadership habits that served them well at the start of the journey and fail to make the necessary adjustments along the way.

## Horses for Courses

To underline the adaptability and interdependence of the Leadership Matters model, the approach one decides to take depends on the situation one is facing. If you take one step further backwards, you will see that your approach is born out of your vision. My time at St Leonard's has involved our whole school team realising two separate visions of the future and we are just embarking upon the third. At our first vision evening, whilst we created a new mission statement and strapline, the image that I presented to those present was one of a fortress. Six years later, the fortress analogy was replaced by a cathedral. Three years after that, we've begun to sail west. Looking at the mathematics of these analogies, one can see that it takes time to make a sustained and sustainable difference to a school. One can also see that once the *heavy work* has been done, momentum can swiftly build. The second vision was realised in half the time that it took the first one to be achieved. The Leadership Matters book refers to Jim Collins' "flywheel concept" taken from his book, *Good to Great*. This resonates exactly with the development model at St Leonard's.

## The Fortress

As a new headteacher it is only natural that, whilst one can see exciting opportunities, one is also able to sense the dangers. The awesome responsibility of the role can increase not only your personal vulnerability but also that of the school. Your leadership needs to get off to a strong start.

I referred to some broken relationships in the *Emerging Truths* section in chapter two. This had certainly led to fractured walls within the organisation. Moreover, the curriculum lacked cohesion and assessment, as far as I could see, was over-reliant on testing. Whilst data was literally everywhere, it was not being used effectively to improve standards. Added into the mix was the imminent prospect of inspection. Remember, the school was officially *good* and had always been such.

I'm hoping that you can see why I chose the image of a fortress as the basis of the vision. If we didn't tighten up and position ourselves correctly, the inspection would definitely breach our barricades. Given the time pressure upon us, our formation was definitely one of defence.

The inspection itself arrived five months into my headship (four if you discount the summer holiday). I referred in the previous chapter to having some good fortune in my leadership. This was certainly manifested in the inspector leading that inspection. I am grateful for his ability to see the situation for what it was and for his willingness to have faith in my fledgling leadership of the school. We retained our *good* – but it was only by the width of a cigarette paper because he said as much.

## Getting Help

Whatever confidence you have in your own ability it is important to accept from the beginning that you cannot achieve all that you wish to in isolation. I was fortunate enough to have an experienced head teacher act as a mentor in my first year of headship. I also benefited from having a truly fantastic school improvement partner from the Local Authority.

In his book, *Imperfect Leadership,* Steve Munby says, *"Imperfect leaders know that they don't have all the answers – they ask for help."* The head teachers I recognise to be the most frazzled by the job are those who try and take on too much themselves in some mistaken belief that everything is down to them. Once when I questioned why someone hadn't asked for help, I received this response: *"Simon, it's alright for you. Your school's outstanding."* For a moment, let's park the fact that this remark displays a distorted view of the purpose of schools and focus on the main misunderstanding.

The fact that St Leonard's was judged to be outstanding in 2017 was not as a result of superhero action coming from me. It was because, firstly, talent within the organisation was appropriately deployed and its brilliance unleashed and secondly, we went anywhere we needed to and asked anyone with the required expertise to come and help us. Our fortress was not fortified by ourselves alone. It was underpinned by the expertise and good will of others. So how was this fortress built?

## Early Years

The first stage of building our fortress involved focusing on the Early Years Foundation Stage. I cannot write this book without engaging in one *soap box* paragraph:

I believe that the Early Years is the most important phase to get consistently right within a primary school. If standards are not at their highest in this phase, then no matter what talent lies elsewhere within your organisation, the children will not achieve as highly as they possibly could. Moreover, Early Years is the phase most misunderstood and undervalued, certainly by politicians and, shamefully by some school leaders. If I was head teacher of a fictitious school and was only allowed one outstanding teacher, I would want them to be in Early Years. Early Years is where the magic begins so you need a magician not a babysitter.

I referred in the previous chapter to the challenge faced by opening a Nursery and two form entry Reception provision in what turned out to be six months before our 2017 inspection. Whilst it's important to acknowledge the quality of the Early Years practice before this time, it was clear that we were not in a position to go from brand new to outstanding by ourselves. So, we sought help.

It's important as a school leader to build networks based on trust and mutual support with other school leaders. The head teacher of the school where my wife was working as a Specialist Leader of Education (SLE) for Early Years allowed her to come and direct and support my newly formed team. This other school was also part of our church school cluster and we have joined together to share in our Leadership Matters journey ever since. The talent of the SLE along with the work ethic and potential talent of the new team meant that progress was rapid. If there's one thing that I am both amazed and impressed by about our inspection outcome, it is that the transformation of our Early Years provision happened so quickly. That's what talent and hard work can achieve.

## Curriculum

Another key ingredient in building our fortress was completely changing our curriculum. In 2017, St Leonard's became an accredited IPC school. The International Primary Curriculum is suited to our school's context. As a school which is around 23% white British, we felt it important that we had a curriculum which was relevant to all of our pupils all of the time. Each unit of work has an international element to it. It is a curriculum which is rooted in personal goals as well as subject goals. Most importantly, it is absolutely focused on teaching and learning important knowledge and skills. The teacher most suited to leading this whole school development was brought onto the leadership team and we launched our new approach in the September of 2012. This book is not about the virtues of the IPC (though there are many and I wouldn't consider using anything else) so the simplest thing to say which does it justice is that it's the only initiative that has been brought in without a single dissenting voice being raised by a staff member, governor, child or parent. If you're reading this as an existing school leader, you'll know that such experiences are very rare indeed!

## Assessment

The development of assessment was a slow journey for us. In the early stages, if I'd asked for an assessment of a child's ability in a core skill I'd have either been given the latest test result or asked to enquire in a couple of weeks after the next test. It wasn't worth asking. We needed help.

In terms of developing English, this was the first external appointment I made to the leadership team. From that point forward, the drive came from within the organisation.

We had our own expert and it was a matter of spreading that expertise throughout the school. With maths, though, we had to go and look for help in developing a relevant mathematics curriculum which had assessment (supported by some testing) at its core. This took a lot of time and we'll visit this example again when we come to the topic of coaching.

## Behaviour

Our fortress had to be built on a foundation of desired behaviour. Sometimes, you just have to play the long game. To be clear, there was not a poor behaviour culture prior to my time at the school. However, there were negative cultural aspects that were clearly visible in a significant minority of the children; laughing at the misfortune of others being the worst of them.

With the elder year groups, we engaged in firefighting when we had to. However, in the youngest groups we spent a lot of time establishing the required behaviours. It is true to say, that with over 100 more pupils in the school today than at that time, we have fewer instances of poor behaviour now than years ago.

## Recruitment

The final element to our fortress building is unsurprisingly our staff. When I walk the corridors of our school today, I am filled with both gratitude and admiration for the people who work there. As a school leader you need to remember that the hopes, dreams and aspirations you have for the school are built upon the talent of those whom you lead. Without them, the school is little, and you are even less. As mentioned about creating teams in chapter four, the key to any appointment to the staff team is that you are both looking to create diversity and keep togetherness. Part of our approach is that it is not exclusively senior leaders which sit on appointment panels on all occasions. The team is everything. You can be an extrovert or an introvert. You can be logical or emotional. You just have to commit to serving others as well as helping yourself.

## The Cathedral

The successful 2017 inspection outcome in conjunction with our accredited IPC school status prompted the need for us to change our vision. The fortress had been built and done its job. It was now time for us to become a cathedral. Let's take a moment to look at the comparison.

The purpose of a fortress is to keep people safely in whilst keeping others out. The purpose of a cathedral is to draw people in from the outside and then to send them out inspired to do better. As an IPC school we welcome practitioners from all over the world into our community. We share our practice and we learn from each other. Our curriculum leader serves on accreditation teams for other IPC schools. As a Church of England (C of E) school, we've undertaken projects to share different elements of our school's practice at both diocesan and national level. In terms of whole school leadership, we've hosted a webinar for the C of E NPQH programme looking at how school and church can work effectively together. We'll look at this in the epilogue.

The past three years has seen us progress from looking at ourselves to looking out for others. In so doing, we are serving the profession as well as ourselves. Remembering that good leaders don't create followers, they create more leaders, teachers have gone from *doing their job* to *leading*.

As you can see in the Buck diagram based on Goleman's leadership styles, once your team is at a phase of achieving excellence, there is far less need for directive and pacesetting styles of leadership. Your role as a whole school leader is now to show confidence in your team by becoming more democratic (without compromising on your non-negotiables) and in individuals by taking a coaching approach. This is both the foundation of the Leadership Matters model and is indeed an end goal to develop in all aspects of leadership. It is through coaching that we can discover abilities within ourselves that we didn't know we possessed. It is through coaching that we help someone to turn their own light on.

## Coaching

When our cluster group works with Andy Buck, coaching is at the heart of his approach and it is also at the heart of our learning. We in turn are practising our coaching skills. The Leadership Matters book refers to GROWTH coaching and Andy has subsequently released his book, *BASIC Coaching* (2020), which offers a fresh approach. These models are summarised below.

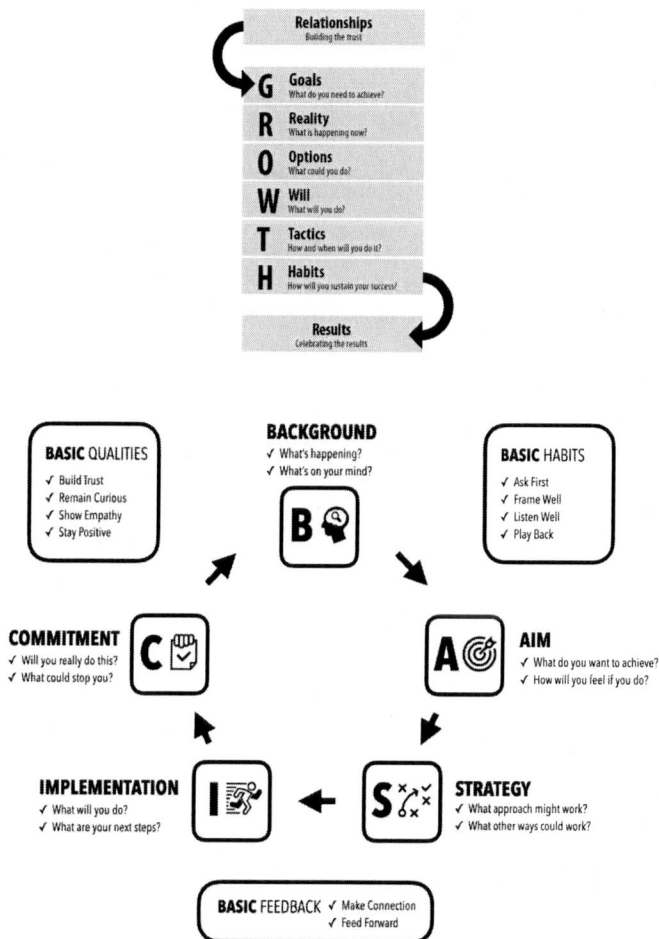

**Relationships**
Building the trust

**G Goals**
What do you need to achieve?

**R Reality**
What is happening now?

**O Options**
What could you do?

**W Will**
What will you do?

**T Tactics**
How and when will you do it?

**H Habits**
How will you sustain your success?

**Results**
Celebrating the results

**BASIC** QUALITIES
✓ Build Trust
✓ Remain Curious
✓ Show Empathy
✓ Stay Positive

**BACKGROUND**
✓ What's happening?
✓ What's on your mind?

**B**

**BASIC** HABITS
✓ Ask First
✓ Frame Well
✓ Listen Well
✓ Play Back

**COMMITMENT**
✓ Will you really do this?
✓ What could stop you?

**C**

**A** **AIM**
✓ What do you want to achieve?
✓ How will you feel if you do?

**IMPLEMENTATION**
✓ What will you do?
✓ What are your next steps?

**I**

**S** **STRATEGY**
✓ What approach might work?
✓ What other ways could work?

**BASIC** FEEDBACK ✓ Make Connection
✓ Feed Forward

As a Leadership Matters case study, this book is not so much about how to coach but rather the impact that it has had on individuals as well as on the organisation as a whole.

An example of how both individual leadership and subject development has benefited from support facilitated by structured conversations involves the development of our whole school approach to mathematics. In 2017 we were able to appoint a new maths leader to the senior leadership team from within our existing team of teachers. As with previous appointments, it was made on the basis of character and general ability rather than declared mathematical expertise. At the time, I still didn't feel that our overall approach to maths assessment was correct. I wanted to build upon the excellent observation-based practice in Early Years to a model which was consistent in approach across the school and could be supported by testing rather than decided by it.

We worked with a brilliant maths consultant. She took time to build a relationship with the maths leader and to demonstrate her own expertise. She supported the leader with tasks such as work scans. They carried out learning walks together. They looked at the maths curriculum and the associated long- and medium-term planning together. They engaged in conversations with teachers together. The consultant carried out demonstrations and engaged in team teaching. At this stage, she was definitely acting in the role of mentor rather than coach.

Leadership Matters explains that whilst mentoring involves you telling or advising someone how to do something, coaching involves asking questions of a person in a way that helps them to discover the way forward for themselves. In this example, the maths consultant had to gauge when to move from a position of mentoring to one of coaching.

Having a mentor, as mentioned at the beginning of this chapter, can be hugely beneficial. There is one hazard to avoid, however. If one is not careful, not only can someone become over-reliant upon the mentor, but they can also begin to think less about their own leadership. This creates a doubly negative consequence. Your school's capacity for leadership is diminished and the mentor can end up with more tasks to do – *the monkey on the back* as described in Leadership Matters.

I remember one conversation with the consultant at the end of a day's visit. From what she'd said, it was clear that, using the GROWTH model, we'd got as far as the *Options* stage. In her opinion, now was the time for her to adopt a coaching role rather than a mentoring one. She had astutely identified that if she didn't step back, she would end up being the decision maker and, of course, part of being a leader involves making a decision, committing to it and being prepared to be held accountable for the decision you've made.

Since this time, not only has the maths leader been able to take complete charge of our school's mathematical provision and develop meaningful assessment, she is now able to hold coaching conversations of her own with members of our teaching team.

Coaching has become central to our working culture at St Leonard's. It is used as part of everyone's appraisal where fewer targets and action plans are centrally driven. Our Early Years leader is also a coach for our NPQML participants. When mentoring NQTs also, if appropriate, the mentor moves into a coaching role if the NQT is able to benefit.

Ultimately, coaching develops self-confidence, resilience, proficiency and above all, the ability to lead well. Relationships improve and as they do, so do standards.

## Sailing West
Leading a school always involves an element of risk. There have been several occasions in my headship where I've been left to reflect that something could have gone either way. If your school is not getting the basics right, then you're unlikely to deviate from a tried and tested formula in getting your school to a position that is stable and healthy.

As confidence grows and standards rise, that is when one is in a position to experiment and take calculated risks. As the Leadership Matters model illustrates, the right actions carried out with the right approach will ultimately deliver great outcomes. But what do you do once that has been achieved? Some might say that this is the time when you may question as a whole school leader if it's time to move on. This could be the case but not necessarily so.

Jocelyn Davis in *The Greats on Leadership* uses a beautifully described analogy involving a shipping company using the established eastern trade routes. Change leadership requires a different approach from visionary leadership. Though they are related, once the course has been set, it is down to the ship's captain to navigate the squalls, tides and the rocks. Once a safe route has been established, there is no perceived need for change because they are profiting from the way they do things. But the visionary is always seeking new opportunities. The visionary is wondering *"What riches might we find if we sail west?"*

Davis says, *"Organisations may say they want leaders to champion new opportunities and strategies, but whenever someone proposes sailing west, there is always a crowd ready to defend their interest in sailing east."*

As the Sigmoid Curve showed in the previous chapter, if all one does is chart the same course, there is inevitable decline to follow. Life is not one monotonous cycle of repetition. It is a voyage of discovery. As the saying goes, *"we sail sometimes with the wind, sometimes with the wind against us; but we must sail."*

For us at St Leonard's, our decision to join the Southwark Diocesan Board of Education Multi Academy Trust was the beginning of our voyage west. It would have been very easy to stay as we were, a voluntary aided school within a Local Authority. A ship's captain cannot be certain of every decision they make. Even along established routes, conditions can swiftly change. For us, I felt that instead of sailing purposefully in calm waters, we were likely to start drifting if we didn't change course.

As such, I took on the role of persuader and was very well supported by the school's governing body. Part of this act of persuasion involved explaining why only two years previously, I had declared opposition to the prospect of joining such a Trust. Therein lies another key leadership lesson. When the circumstances change, one may have to change one's views on something. Our decision to join was unanimous. It was not based on any political view. It was purely based on the question, *"What is right for our school now?"* Whilst we encountered noisy but hollow opposition from one union in particular, our staff and our parents supported the decision. I'm not going to pretend that academy conversion doesn't involve choppy waters; it most certainly does. But we are beginning to reap the rewards of embarking upon this new voyage. Leaders at all levels are beginning to form teams within a Trust in the same way as we did as a school. It will take time. We've a new journey to make and I've every confidence that the school will make it.

St Leonard's is a school with a rich history. We'll explore in the next chapter how we've used our history to impact upon our present. For now, though, take some time to reflect on the voyage that you are currently embarked upon.

Here are some questions which you may find helpful.
- ∞ What leadership style is required of you at the moment?
- ∞ Do you need to use different styles for different people or groups?
- ∞ Where are you on the voyage of realising your vision?
- ∞ Does your vision need to be modified or radically changed?
- ∞ Who needs mentoring and who needs coaching in your setting?
- ∞ Who could coach you?
- ∞ Do you need to sail east or west?

# 7

# Build Upon the Rock

---

*"Deep in their roots, all flowers keep the light."*
**Theodore Roosevelt**

As you will have read, the Leadership Matters model starts with looking at yourself and your situation. However, whether your school has been newly formed or has a history such as St Leonard's which spans over 200 years, there's a story which should act as the foundation of your leadership; the reason your school exists. It is the fire inside. It is the light which you need to shine today in order to bear witness to those deeply rooted values.

Any vision and subsequent strategy introduced by you should not only reflect your personal values and the current situation, but the historic values of the organisation. This needs to be made explicit to everyone within your community. Whether it's about how you recruit staff or how you share it with children through your curriculum, whatever your school's story is, discover it, reveal it and share it. It will serve you well, especially when the tough times arrive as it will keep you centred. A shared love of a school's history and foundation is just part of what I believe to be the difference between a good school and an excellent one.

**A Common Misunderstanding**

Church of England (C of E) schools are often mistakenly classified as *"faith schools"* instead of simply *"Church schools."* Let me explain. The rationale behind the establishment of C of E schools was to provide education for the poor within each parish rather than to explicitly teach the Christian faith. When the National Society was formed in 1812 (without Tchaikovsky's overture, I think!), C of E schools began to exist some 20 years or so prior to the establishment of what we would now consider to be state education. Church of England schools are Christian in their foundation, but they are not schools exclusively for Christians.

This compares and contrasts with the foundation of Roman Catholic, Jewish, Sikh or Islamic schools for example, which are indeed faith schools as they were established to specifically teach those faiths and overwhelmingly provide for children and families from within their faith.

**Our Foundation**

Like many great ideas, the St Leonard's story began in a pub. Since those early days in the rooms above a coaching yard behind the White Lion pub in Streatham, the school building has migrated on at least two further occasions to the site it rests on now a few thousand yards away. As a leader, there are many times when I wish it was back behind the pub! Our goal today remains the same as it did over 200 years ago – to serve our community, especially its poorest; to inspire children to succeed whilst nurturing their talent within the Christian tradition.

Our past is at the heart of our identity. It is lived in our present and it inspires us to work for a better future. It is precisely because of our foundation that I wrote this letter to our school community on the day our Ofsted inspection report was published in 2017:

*Dear all,*

*I am now able to share the final report from our recent school inspection. Ofsted have judged the school to be "outstanding" in all categories.*

*I would like to take this opportunity to thank the staff, governors, children and their families for their sustained contribution in helping our school to be awarded this judgment and for their contribution to the inspection itself.*

*I have stated many times that I recognise that Ofsted has a duty to categorise our school, but that we are not defined or limited by their conclusions. Instead, we are defined by our Christian foundation, by our 204 years of history, by our own vision and by our own core purpose of giving our children the best that we can in order to prepare them for their independent futures. As such, whilst I'm certainly very pleased with the outcome, my job is to ensure that we continue to improve. Those working within the school will take the chance to celebrate this successful outcome, but we will do so in the spirit of thanksgiving rather than triumph. All schools have changes in performance at different periods in their history – so there will be no "Ofsted Outstanding" banner hanging over our railings because, whilst that may be who we currently are, it will never be who we are or why we're here.*

*Nevertheless, I naturally take great pleasure in supplying you with this report, as it serves as a witness to the dedication and talent of our fantastic staff, the work of our children and the support of our governors, parents and whole school community. I also recognise the significance of the fact that this is the first time in the 25 years since Ofsted were formed that St Leonard's has been awarded this grade. As such, the wider community can be rightly proud of its school and I can only apologise if the local house prices go up!*

*It is my privilege to serve this school community and to lead its staff. This moment is for you and for all those past and present who consider St Leonard's to be a special part of their lives.*

*Congratulations!*

*Kind regards,*
*Mr Simon Jackson*
*Head Teacher*

## Institutional Success

The best leaders are ambitious more for their organisation than for themselves. The joy comes in achieving shared goals rather than personal accolades. When success comes, it is for the glory of the institution rather than the individual. It is your job as a school leader to reflect achievement rather than absorb it. Success should be benchmarked against the school's values, standards and expectations. To try and live up to another organisation's values is to begin to stop leading. This leads us, somewhat inevitably to the matter of Ofsted.

## Ofsted

As my letter implies, to attempt to lead a school for the benefit of Ofsted is to take on a mission which is doomed to fail. You are leading for your school community. If Ofsted has been given authority and power by government, it is true to say that many school leaders have erroneously enhanced this further by becoming a slave to the inspectorate. As mentioned in chapter one, you need to stand for something.

I write this book as a serving inspector. This has become part of what I do. It is not, however, a role which defines who I am. Ofsted has a duty to judge whether a school's provision adequately meets the needs of children and their families. It is impossible though for any visitor, however well qualified, to come to know a school's heart and soul over a couple of days. That is not Ofsted's purpose. Reflect on how your school managed the coronavirus pandemic; how you served your community. I hope that your leadership intent was purely based on what you thought was best to meet the needs of your children at the time. I doubt very much if you consulted the Ofsted framework.

Ofsted stopped inspecting schools during the pandemic. Its core purpose was not matched to the needs of our country and its schools at the time, and that is not in any way to be taken as a criticism. I state it to emphasise the fact that it is the school's core values which are most relevant in times of challenge.

One or two less than gracious individuals have suggested that a school graded outstanding under a previous framework is unlikely to be judged so under a present one. We'll see. Anyhow – so what? We don't lead for Ofsted and to be fair to them, they don't ask us to. We lead for our community. We lead for our teams. We lead for the children. We lead because we believe in the school's foundation and wish to uphold its ethos and fulfil its mission. An Ofsted grade is theirs to give and theirs to take away. It does not in any way diminish the contribution made by a school leader if they have truly lived out the school's values to the best of their ability. If your leadership isn't good enough without the outstanding Ofsted grade, it certainly won't be enough with it.

Leadership Matters is completely the right approach for you to adopt if your heart and mind believes that your personal leadership values can be transformative for a school community. If this resonates with you, then you are likely to succeed in many ways, including with inspection outcomes. But Leadership Matters is not a guide on how to succeed in inspection.

### Be Inspired

Before schools closed due to coronavirus, a letter I wrote to parents included these words:

*You will no doubt be aware of the announcement made by the Secretary of State for Education that schools are to close from tomorrow afternoon and will largely remain closed until further notice to the vast majority of pupils. A phrase I've heard a lot over the past few weeks is, "These are unprecedented times." This may be true for some countries and for some schools, but it is most definitely not the case for our United Kingdom or for this school. Some 10 million soldiers died in World War One – 30,000 in one hour alone in 1916. 37 former staff and pupils of this school lost their lives. As such, we really need to keep a sense of perspective. This is a sad time; an extraordinary time – but it is our time and we need to step up and be the teachers and parents our children need.*

I have been inspired by the leadership of a previous headmaster (as titled at the time) of St Leonard's. The delightfully named Henry Crumbleholme led the school from 1900 until 1933. He stayed loyal to the school during its most troubled times. He was a true visionary who not only preserved the school's existence by making it co-educational in the 1920s, but also in 1933, the year of his retirement, gave us the school crest as we know it today. That was leadership in difficult circumstances. Our main hall has been renamed in his honour.

In the same way, we've honoured significant individuals in the school's history by naming different rooms in the modern building after them. These include the school's founder, the school's first head mistress (along with a roll call of female school leaders) and a single family which had three members of it leading the school at different stages in its history. We make our children aware not only about what has happened in our school's history but who was involved. A child does not just come to St Leonard's to learn. They come to be part of a 200 years old story, to contribute to that story and we hope that the values of the school stay with them for the rest of their lives.

## Anchored

In the last chapter, we looked at sailing west to seek new opportunities. To keep the analogy, there are times when a ship needs to be anchored for its own benefit. In the same way that we're inspired by our history, as I mentioned in chapter three, we are also now looking to both seek new opportunities and return to our foundation by walking in the steps of St Leonard himself. As such, we're working in partnership with our parish church to use what we grow in our school vegetable garden to help support the Nehemiah project, which operates a halfway house for reformed prisoners. We are also going to be supporting the *first touch* charity which helps sick and premature babies at St George's hospital in south London. Our past foundation is being lived once more in the present.

## The Rock

On hearing the words, *"the rock"*, one thinks of imposing images such as Gibraltar or Alcatraz. A Christian may think of Jesus' words to Peter which you can read about in the epilogue of this book. For our school, Leadership Matters has also been a rock. The title and the image on the cover of this book encourages you to look to the light - but do not ignore the value of the rock. It is the rock which supports everything. There will be plenty of times in your leadership when you will have to show your firm resolve before people will be able to see the light. The rock is your school's foundation and it defines your mission. The light brought forth from this foundation sends you out and brings you safely home.

Here are some questions which may help you:
∞ What about your school's history excites you?
∞ What about your school's foundation needs to be shared with the wider school community?
∞ What are the school's historic values and how will you live them out in your leadership?
∞ What is the rock that underpins your vision?
∞ Who do you lead for?
∞ When do you need to be the rock and when do you need to be the light?

# 8

# Hope Springs Eternal

*"When you know what you hope for most and hold it like a light within you, you can make things happen, almost like magic."*
**Laini Taylor**

All endings are a chance to rest, to breathe, to reflect on the conclusion of a journey in preparation for a new one. As the main body of this book comes to an end, I hope that in reflecting upon what you've read, you will be able to connect with the Leadership Matters model in a new way. If you are inspired to act on the voice inside your head which is calling you to lead, that would be even better. This may be the time for a new beginning for you. It may be time to sail west. At the very least, I hope that this book will help you on your current voyage of discovery.

When starting this project with Andy, it began with my choice of book title and the writing of the blurb. Andy then set about creating various cover designs. These ranged from very literal images such as an actual light bulb being turned on to various pastoral images where the light shone through.

## Prepare to Fly

The final design was ultimately chosen as it encapsulates for me not only what this book is about but what leadership in general involves. I've already referred to both the light and the rock in the image as well as sailing analogies. As yet though, I haven't mentioned the flock of geese. Leadership Matters fans will naturally identify geese as being the branded logo for the movement. Those of you who follow Andy on Twitter will know that he often uses the hashtag *#honk* to offer encouragement to other leaders in the same way as the geese in formation honk to encourage the goose at the head of the flock. However, whilst both of these references are relevant, they are by no means the only reasons for the importance of their inclusion.

Leadership is synonymous with flight and journeys. The American author, C Joybell C is quoted as saying:

*"I have come to accept the feeling of not knowing where I am going. And I have trained myself to love it. Because it is only when we are suspended in mid-air with no landing in sight, that we force our wings to unravel and alas begin our flight. And as we fly, we still may not know where we are going to. But the miracle is in the unfolding of the wings. You may not know where you're going, but you know that so long as you spread your wings, the winds will carry you."*

This may seem to be slightly at odds with all that we've considered in terms of the need for having a vision, communicating it clearly, creating your teams, devising a strategy and then delivering on it. However, it absolutely shows an understanding of life as a leader, both its joys and its sorrows. Sometimes things happen and they can happen without warning. There have been many times in my headship when I've been left to reflect that I've been fortunate not to have had to endure certain experiences which other head teachers have. School leadership is hard because there is so much of it that is outside of your control. It can often feel like being *suspended in mid-air with no landing in sight*. However, from my perspective, headship is also the biggest privilege as well as the biggest responsibility. The miracle is indeed in the unfolding of the wings. With the Leadership Matters approach to support you, you will be able to travel a long distance with confidence and crucially carry others with you.

## Lead for Others

Whilst leaders should most definitely be *doers* in times of crisis, they should be *enablers* for a great deal of the time. Your focus should always be on others rather than yourself (this does not mean that you neglect yourself or drive yourself into the ground). A Leader as described by Napoleon, *"is a dealer in hope."* The quality of your leadership will be defined by how well you serve others and how successfully you can help them to see the light. You must always be seen as a torch bearer and yet allow others to kindle your flame and pick up that torch. Not only must you set the ship's course to reach the destination, but you must also carry the lifejackets.

Jocelyn Davis sums it up beautifully and bluntly:

*"Good leaders step forward when others stay back. They speak when others stay silent. They forge ahead where no path has been forged, and they set an example for others to follow. You won't always see them out in front; often they are found working alongside their team or taking up a position in the wings so their people can shine in the spotlight. But wherever they choose to stand at a particular moment, it won't be against a wall, butt covered, observing which way the wind blows."*

## The Importance of Legacy

One thing I've reflected on since we transitioned from the 20th to the 21st century is the importance of leadership sustainability in a world which seems to be focused so much more on instant remedies and transient values. The pace of career progression has certainly increased since I entered the profession in 1993. I deliberately chose to gain experience in all primary year groups before becoming a deputy head teacher. I had 17 years' career experience before I became a head teacher. Everyone's journey is different and the current recruitment and retention challenge in the profession has necessitated a lot of this change in pace. As such, an important part of your role as a whole school leader involves leaving a legacy of leadership that endures.

I wonder if Henry Crumbleholme ever imagined in 1933, that not quite a century later, his influence would still remain at St Leonard's? I'm not suggesting for one moment that existing head teachers should have statues of themselves placed inside the school gates or dedicate the school library in their own name, but we do have a duty to leave a legacy of some kind. So what should this look like?

Firstly, it seems obvious, but it's important that you leave the school in a better position than you came to it. More than this, however, it's important that you leave the school in a position to become better than it currently is. Other than that, within the school itself one has to recognise one's limitations. In the early days of my headship, when there was clearly a lot of work to be done, I was wisely told by the deputy head teacher at the time (who retired in 2019 after 25 years' service at the school), *"Remember, Simon - you can only write a chapter; you can't write the whole book."*

In a recent virtual meeting with the teaching team, I invited them to reflect on the fact that their contribution to the education of our children during the coronavirus pandemic was both ground-breaking and history making. Considering the circumstances, it will be classed as the most challenging period for schools since their enforced closure during World War Two. As such, we decided to create a time capsule that will stand as a testament to the events of 2020. The legacy of their contribution during this challenging moment in our history will endure for a far greater period than our successful Ofsted inspection for example. They have all shown leadership and their leadership has mattered.

I've come to realise that in the modern age, your legacy as a leader depends upon the impact your leadership has upon the philosophies and careers of others. Remember, leaders don't create followers, they create other leaders. I will only know how successful I've been when I discover how many of the current team at the school, particularly its female leaders, go on to achieve their desired career progression.

### Leaving the light on

One of the most powerful experiences I've had as an adult was visiting the Anne Frank house and museum in Amsterdam. It's unlike any other experience I've had. There's a unique atmosphere and a sense of what took place there remains. Among many poignant entries in her diary are these words:

*"It's really a wonder that I haven't dropped all my ideals, because they seem so absurd and impossible to carry out. Yet I keep them, because in spite of everything, I still believe that people are really good at heart."*

Most of us will never come close to leaving a legacy such as Anne's. That's ok. You may be at a stage in your life and career when it seems as if all you want to achieve is far away, or that either people or the requirements of our education system stand for values which are very different from your own. Like Anne, do not drop your ideals. For however absurd or impossible the chances of realising them may seem at the moment, they are why your leadership matters. They will provide you with light in the darkest of times and they will become the guiding light for others. This brings us back to where we started. Stand for something or you'll fall for anything. What are you going to stand for? Why? Who will you stand with?

Writing *Leave A Light On* and sharing it with you has been a privilege and a joy. In reading this book, thank you for allowing my thoughts and words to spend some time within your mind. I hope that at least something has resonated with you.

May I gently invite you to read the epilogue. It looks at each of the chapters you've read from the position of a church school leader. It is not theologically profound. It is not written as a call to convert. It is merely an invitation to reflect on your leadership from a different perspective.

We live and work in a world which is so fast moving, where so often we don't have the time to reflect on what really matters, so as this book comes to an end, I'll share these words of Robert Fulghum in his book, *All I Really Need to Know I Learned in Kindergarten: Uncommon Thoughts On Common Things* (1988):

*"I believe that imagination is stronger than knowledge. That myth is more potent than history. That dreams are more powerful than facts. That hope always triumphs over experience. That laughter is the only cure for grief. And I believe that love is stronger than death."*

I wish you well in your leadership journey. Your leadership matters. Commit to your vision and values. Build your teams wisely. Create allies. Cherish friends. Take time to enjoy success, learn from failure… and always leave a light on.

# Epilogue

## Christian Reflections for Leaders of Church Schools

*"The light shines in the darkness, and the darkness has not overcome it.*
**John 1:5**

In this epilogue, we will be looking at leadership from a Christian perspective through the lens of the Church of England. We will follow the chapter headings of *Leave A Light On* so as to follow the progression of the Leadership Matters model. How you use this epilogue is up to you. It can be read in isolation or you can visit the relevant section before or after reading a chapter of the book. It is written with the intent of providing an opportunity for you to reflect on your philosophy, your values and yourself as an individual leader. It is also written with an understanding that the leadership values referred to are not exclusively Christian in their nature. However, the message of the Bible is at the heart of this section of the book. As such, if you are a leader within a

Church of England school, you may wish to take on the additional task of considering, either individually or in discussion with your leadership team, how the approach of the Church is aligned to your own vision, values and strategy within your setting.

# Standing for Something

*"Let your light shine before others, that they may see your good deeds and glorify your Father in heaven."*
**Matthew 5:15-16**

## Church of England vision

The Church of England has the following statement on its website:

Our *(Church of England)* vision for education is deeply Christian, with Jesus' promise of 'life in all its fullness' at its heart.

In line with the Church of England's role as the established Church, our vision is for the common good of the whole community.

**Educating for wisdom, knowledge and skills:** enabling discipline, confidence and delight in seeking wisdom and knowledge, and developing talents in all areas of life.

**Educating for hope and aspiration:** enabling healing, repair and renewal, coping wisely when things go wrong, opening horizons and guiding people into ways of fulfilling them.

**Educating for community and living well together:** a core focus on relationships, participation in communities and the qualities of character that enable people to flourish together.

**Educating for dignity and respect:** the basic principle of respect for the value and preciousness of each person, treating each person as a unique individual of inherent worth.

*"The Christian faith is about a vision for society as well as individuals – it's about how we can live well in all our relationships and communities. In a world where many visions for humanity compete for our attention, the Church asks: what do the great questions of our age, national and local, look like if you view them through the prism of the gospel?"*

So, what does the Church of England stand for? Similarly, what are the great questions of our age in relation to leadership?

The Church of England's Foundation for Educational Leadership has published a document titled *Called Connected Committed* by Ford and Wolfe (2020) in which they look at 24 leadership practices for education leaders. The mission of the Foundation is *"To develop inspirational leaders who are called, connected and committed to delivering the Church of England's vision for education."*

## Humility and Authenticity

The Leadership Matters model starts with looking at your personal qualities. Personal qualities are naturally important to the church school leader. Ford and Wolfe state that, *"Leaders in education know that humility is intrinsic to authenticity. They acknowledge their own imperfections, take responsibility for their mistakes and shine a light on other people's successes. Their choice to serve others builds trust and enables genuine collaboration. Whether rejoicing in success or dealing with failure, they pursue love, around which everything turns and towards which everything should be drawn."*

This idea of authenticity as a leader is central also to the Leadership Matters model. Whilst we will always be imperfect, we can only succeed if we are being true to ourselves. If we do not know ourselves and cannot be ourselves, then we are not well placed to serve others. In accepting ourselves for who we are, we have to trust that this will be enough. As Ford and Wolfe delightfully put it, *"God does not always call the equipped, but does equip the called."*

## Looking at yourself

In chapter one of this book, I look at myself based on the light being shed from the personal profiling tool, LM Persona. But what does the Bible offer me in the way of personal reflection?

My Christian names are Simon Thomas. Unfortunately, my mother is no longer with us for her to be able to be held answerable for her choice, but I think that chapter 20 of John's Gospel reveals her to be both scarily intuitive and also accountable for at least some of the blame for my character!

John 20 begins with Mary Magdalene visiting the empty tomb on the morning of the resurrection. She then goes and tells Simon Peter and another disciple that the stone has been moved away from the tomb. Although Simon is not first to arrive, he goes in straight away without thinking. Later in the chapter, Jesus appears to his remaining disciples, all except Thomas. When the disciples tell Thomas about what has occurred, he refuses to believe them. *"Unless I see…I will not believe"* he says.

There are several occasions in the gospel when Simon Peter is seen to be acting impulsively and there's enough contained within the opening chapter of this book for you to see how I can identify with him. As for Thomas, at the end of John 20, Jesus says to him, *"Blessed are those who have not seen and yet have believed."* Thomas is known to many as *the doubter* and, as a school leader, I have a lot of empathy with him.

School leaders work constantly in the realm of doubt. The education system makes it so. Consider the aspect of school accountability for example. Schools, as Steve Munby refers to in his book, *Imperfect Leadership,* are all too often about proving rather than improving. There are those whom, unless they see the league table or the inspection report, they will not believe in the quality of the school. Ironically, they are also often people who don't apply the same approach when they hear negative gossip about the school!

Faith is not necessarily the absence of doubt. Rather, it is the commitment to the journey needing to be made despite the doubt being felt. There will be times in your leadership when you may make a decision on the basis of everyday hope rather than Christian certainty. As a Church school leader, you should be able to rely on the support and prayers of the wider body which is available within the Church community.
Creating faith in your leadership is one of your biggest priorities. Remembering to under promise and over deliver, it's important that you can be open enough to declare why you're there and what you stand for. For as Simon Sinek says in his book, *Start with Why?* (2009), *"people don't buy what you do, they buy why you do it."*

A favourite hymn of my mother's was *Just as I am without one plea.* For me it sums up the journey of faith and doubt beautifully. Ultimately, it comes down to our willingness or not to believe in a promise. As a reflection for this chapter, contemplate these verses below.

*Just as I am, though tossed about*
*With many a conflict, many a doubt*
*Fighting and fears within without*
*O Lamb of God, I come, I come*

*Just as I am, Thou wilt receive*
*Wilt welcome, pardon, cleanse, relieve*
*Because Thy promise I believe*
*O Lamb of God, I come, I come*

Some questions which may help you with your reflection:
- ∞ Why do you think you've been called to leadership?
- ∞ Who are you connected with?
- ∞ What are you committed to?
- ∞ Who in the stories of the Bible do you relate to? Why?
- ∞ Where are you in your leadership journey of faith or doubt?

# In the beginning

*"And God said, "Let there be light," and there was light."*
**Genesis 1:3**

### Control from chaos

When I began at St Leonard's, I was horrified to discover just how many year groups studied the creation story, not only because of the clear issue relating to curriculum mapping, but also due to the potential for theological interpretation being misunderstood as scientific fact. However, creation as a concept is of great importance to a Church school leader. Indeed, one can look at your headship within the context of servant leadership as an act of creation.

The physicist and theologian Dr Lydia Jaeger explained in an interview for *War Cry* in 2014 that, *"The doctrine of creation is fundamental to the Christian understanding of the world. If you believe in creation, you have a very different outlook on the world from somebody who believes that it came about by chance. That insight affects everyday concerns, such as work, the environment and relationships."*

The Leadership Matters model explains a process which leads to the creation of *culture* and *climate*. As we know, the model begins with the leader bringing their personal qualities to a situation and asking themselves, *"What does this situation require of me?"* However, as a Church school leader, this has to involve a sense of responding to God's will which asks: *"What is God asking of me? What is the Christian purpose that is needing to be fulfilled?"* As such, the climate, irrespective of the challenges presented by outside forces, should always include a sense of Christian encouragement – that wherever we are on our journey of faith or doubt, if we are focused on the things which matter - *Thy will be done; Thy kingdom come.*

## Free Will

The doctrine of creation is not to be misunderstood as being dependent upon a literal interpretation of the story as narrated in Genesis. It is, however, to be understood as an act of free will by God.

Jaeger argues, *"Creation is a unique act. The Bible opens with a firm statement: 'In the beginning God created the heavens and the earth.' It doesn't start out with an argument for creation or for the existence of God, it just confronts us with God's presence and his work. It is beyond our understanding, but that doesn't mean it is unreal, rubbish or irrational."*

Chapter Two of *Leave A Light On* amongst other things looks at a school development model from Sir David Carter, in which the four stages *de-clutter, repair, improve and sustain* are explored. The situation that you will be facing when beginning your leadership within a school will not have come about by chance. It will have been created as a result of free will based upon the decisions made by people and relationships which have pre-existed. The repair stage involves you establishing control from chaos, making reactive decisions and creating a sense of normality about your situation. I suggest that instead of taking Genesis as your inspiration, you reflect on the content of the Leadership Matters model and this book, as six years is a slightly more realistic timeline than six days to make the required progress!

## Educating for hope and aspiration

If we return to the vision for education of the Church of England, the second element is *educating for hope and aspiration.* Ford and Wolfe talk of leaders being *"shaped by visionary imagination"* and enabling a *"hope filled future."* An act of creation by the leader which includes an appreciation for the wonder of the world around us is at the heart of this vision. As such, your school's environment should be a priority for your consideration when assessing the situation as you find it. However, there is so much more to consider than the physical environment. An understanding of the human and spiritual environment is also essential in being able to generate both hope and aspiration. You need to acquire a good understanding of the relationships which presently exist if you are to be able to imagine something better being created in the future, which is where both hope and aspiration ultimately reside.

If your vision for education is *deeply Christian, with Jesus' promise of 'life in all its fullness' at its heart* then you need to bring an explicitly Christian approach to both your values and your practice. This is why I turned up at St Leonard's on day one with the fruit of the spirit (Galatians 5:22-23) as the light by which we would all be guided. Whatever the situation is that you are faced with, some or all of these qualities can only serve to make a positive difference *(love, joy, peace, patience, kindness, goodness, gentleness, faithfulness, self-control).*

## Encouragement

Psalm 119:105 reminds us: *"Your word is a lamp for my feet, a light on my path."* It reminds us that the Church school leader does not come to the situation alone. You are not required to create everything by yourself. Along with any personal faith, your local family of Church schools and your diocesan board of education should be able to support you. Should your school be in a parish which has a functioning church within it, the partnership with church can have a hugely positive impact on the fulfilment of your vision to serve God's purpose and your community. We'll look at this later in the epilogue.

## Render to Caesar

Chapter Two of *Leave A Light On* concludes by asking you to consider two elements: *What is important? What is within your control?* Church school leaders can definitely experience conflict in this area when considering the pressures arising from the requirements of our education system and placing them alongside the values we are called to uphold as a Christian community. The changes to the Statutory Inspection of

Anglican and Methodist Schools (SIAMs) Framework in 2018 reflect this well. In the past, some Church schools were being classed as outstanding in their Church school inspection whilst requiring improvement by Ofsted. As such, it's important to remember the purpose of the foundation of our C of E schools: to provide an education for the poor of the parish. Therefore, in order to respond appropriately to your situation, there needs to be an understanding that high standards of teaching and learning are at the heart of the Christian purpose of Church schools. This should always be a priority which remains within your control. However, at the heart of the Church leader's approach should also be a willingness to listen to and reflect on what God's overall purpose is for your school. Anyone looking at your school, regardless of their perspective, should be able to see your school's foundation being actively lived in the present day. That is equally your responsibility.

Some questions which may help you with your reflection:
∞ What are you being called to create within your school?
∞ How do you create a sense of Christian encouragement?
∞ How are you creating and sharing a hope-filled future within your school?
∞ Which of the fruit of the spirit are most / least visible within your school?
∞ Why do you think this is? How will you respond? What will you do?

# Growing Together

*"Commit your works to the Lord and your plans will be established."*
**Proverbs 16:3**

As referred to in the previous section, a key difference in leading a Church school involves asking yourself at every stage (as the vision becomes reality) if you are remaining faithful to the foundation of the school and its Christian purpose. Remember that the Church of England requires its leaders to have a vision which is *"deeply Christian, serving the common good."*

## Creating Alignment

Creating alignment within a Church school setting involves working with children, staff, parents, governors, clergy, congregation, diocesan personnel, Local Authority personnel and community. As this list would imply, it is not a process which can be rushed and it requires clear communication and engagement. This relates to the *connected* section of *Called, Connected, Committed*. It builds on an understanding that if relationships are not right, then the creation of hope and aspiration is going to be negatively affected.

When creating alignment, the aim should be for all members of the school's community to be able to flourish as a result of the decision-making process. Mary Myatt in her book, *Hopeful Schools* (2016) says, *"Everyone has a voice does not mean that anything and everything goes. It is instead an attitude adopted by leaders and adults that things will be done in the best interests of everyone at heart, not that everyone will get their way."*

In my time at St Leonard's, there have been two really significant strategic decisions to make when considering our future. The first one was whether to expand and become a two forms of entry school and the second was whether to join the SDBE's Multi Academy

Trust. A key consideration in our decision making on both occasions was whether our actions would be strengthening our connectedness with the school's foundation or weakening it. This book is not about extoling the virtues or otherwise of expansion or academy conversion. It is though about principles of good leadership. One such principle is that you're always wanting to discover *what* is right rather than *who* is right. As President Harry Truman once said, *"It's amazing what you can accomplish if you do not care who gets the credit."*

### School and Church Partnership

During my headship, I have worked with a Rector already in post, experienced an interregnum and worked with a newly appointed Rector. As such, I have a good frame of reference with which to make comparative judgments and to identify really important elements to develop strongly. Let's briefly explore how to create alignment between the two establishments.

The first thing to say is that in an effective school and church partnership, there is a mutual understanding that the two institutions are interdependent. Human flourishing is better enabled for both church and school when they are closely aligned. Our children are welcomed in the church and our congregation are welcomed in the school. Worship in school is appropriately designed to prepare children for worship in church. The Rector advises on and supports the teaching of RE within the school. There is a strong Church presence on the school's governing body and therefore there is both clear communication between the two partners and a shared knowledge of each other's priorities. Crucially, the partners are involved in the development of each other's mission and this starts at the recruitment stage.

There was strong representation from the church and the diocese on my head teacher appointment panel. This was repeated for the appointment of the new deputy head teacher. This was very much to be expected. What perhaps was less expected and yet delighted me, was the fact that the school was included in the selection process of the new Rector. I participated in the church consultation on drawing up the person specification and a wonderful part of the selection process involved all candidates visiting the school for a tour. It's important as a school leader to remember that a clergy appointment has to be considered in the light of wishing to benefit the wider majority within a parish and not just through the eyes of a child. This being said, it's great when you're consulted because at the very least it demonstrates that children are being thought about. As a result of the new appointment, school and church have become more closely aligned than ever before and we have plans for even greater things in the future.

**Headteacher / Clergy relationship**
The relationship between these two individuals is mightily significant when seeking to create a flourishing community. If there is little alignment in philosophy and practice, this can result in a nominal partnership which bears little fruit and can feel like a battle of wills on occasions. However, when there is a partnership based on reciprocity, an acceptance of difference and a genuine desire to assist each other with the development of life in all its fullness within the parish – then the possibilities are endless.

The Rector and I talk regularly, openly, passionately and confidentially about our vision, mission and outcomes. We are supportive of each other and we care about the success of each other's challenges. It is a totally different relationship from that enjoyed with a school improvement partner or adviser, for example. When it is like this, it is one of the most beneficial differences between Church school and community school leadership. As such, it is a relationship worth investing in for both partners.

**Resilience rather than endurance**
Within a Christian context, *growing together* should not be confused with making continual improvement. Schools are very complex places where human beings are constantly being placed under pressure and, on occasions, multiple pressures.

Ford & Wolfe assert that, *"Jesus' offer of "life in all its fullness" is not rose-tinted or naïve. The Christian life does not offer exemption from challenge, or removal of suffering. Rather it gives us a lens through which to see our challenges and recognises that in our most challenging or painful times, God is at work in us, both as individuals and teams – guiding, strengthening, refining and re-focusing us, enabling us to bounce back stronger."*

I have sometimes seen evidence in school leaders that they have mistaken endurance for resilience. Sometimes, tragically, this has led to a decline in their mental or physical health and has ultimately resulted in a head teacher leaving their position. It is a horrible thing to watch happen and there is an element of helplessness about it because, if someone can't accept that they need help, ultimately their fate is sealed. The etymology of the word "resilience" implies the ability to "leap back". Endurance on the other hand is rooted in prolonged suffering.

The Bible is full of stories which illustrate not only how Jesus suffered, but also how the Christian church suffered in its establishment. It also contains stories explaining how people brought suffering upon themselves as a result of their own actions. It is a hard truth to accept on occasions, that schools and leaders can bring about their own suffering as a result of a lack of togetherness and an inability to seek the common good. Whilst our suffering does not result in a death sentence or persecution *(though some politicians and journalists may like it to be so!),* any wounds which we self-inflict also affect children and our team which is why our leadership matters so much and why it can weigh heavily on occasions.

There will always be an element of endurance in the role of school leader because you are called to serve the whole community: *that* child; *that* parent; *that* teacher; *that* governor. Then there will always be the pressure and scrutiny applied by political forces. Most challengingly, there will be those occasions when things happen, sometimes terrible things, which cannot have been foreseen. But rather than endure, at the heart of Christian understanding is the belief that there is a purpose in our troubles and that God is continuing to equip us, mould us and prepare us for greater days ahead. In this, he provides us with the hope required to continue. It is that hope which transforms endurance into resilience. This hope, allied with faith and love as explained in 1 Corinthians 13 will help you to *bear all things, believe all things, hope all things, endure all things.* Your ultimate challenge as school leader, vision creator and architect is to ensure that you can generate that same level of resilience in your team.

Some questions which may help you with your reflection:
∞ How will you bring your understanding of your relationship with God to your leadership?
∞ Who / What helps you to bear, believe, hope and endure in your current role?
∞ Which do you need to focus on developing: endurance or resilience?

# Amazing Grace

*"I once was lost but now am found; was blind but now I see"*

**John Newton**

I believe that a Christian understanding of grace lies at the heart of the difference between Christian leadership and leadership in other forms. Traditionally understood as *the free and unearned favour of God*, grace does more than save us. It is through grace that we are forgiven, restored, transformed and exalted.

The author of the hymn *Amazing Grace* was John Newton. A former slave trader, he wrote the lyrics in 1772 some years after his conversion to Christianity. Newton declared of his past, *"It will always be a subject of humiliating reflection to me, that I was once an active instrument in a business at which my heart now shudders."*

Just as we've reflected on and understood that our powers of resilience and endurance will be tested in many ways, there is nothing which prevents us from being restored through God's grace and mercy. This is important as a leader of a Church school because we can see our many imperfections and the times when we have fallen short, not as failures but as part of the process by which we are redeemed. Similarly, when we experience success, we will be less prone to arrogance because we will also be acutely aware of what we've been saved from.

When we are aware of how grace has been shown towards us, we are called to show that grace to others; and it's hard sometimes! When we are able look with grace, we are able to see the best in others. We are also able to empathise with their imperfections and communicate openly and supportively with them. This is when the power of status and job role are removed because we can communicate as equals – and that's when real progress can happen.

## Healing Relationships

It's no secret that Christian communities are no less averse to having disagreements based on sincerely held positions. It is important that different views are shared openly for it is far harder to create alignment when conversations are taking place in the shadows. Difference needs to be brought into the light.

We are all human and it wouldn't be fair to judge a Christian's humanity differently from others. Nonetheless, Christian leaders are called to *leave a light on* by engaging in a journey of healing for the benefit of the common good. Compassion and forgiveness are required. However, what do these characteristics look like from a Church school leader's perspective?

## Compassion

The word *compassion* originates from the Latin *compati* meaning *"to suffer with."* As such, at its heart, having compassion implies that the person you are showing such feeling towards has actually suffered. It is not about excusing the inexcusable and failing to hold someone to account based on their feelings. It is an emotion that as a leader is rooted in empathy rather than (as it may be for a friend) sympathy.

This is a tough judgment to get consistently right – and I am certainly not claiming to do so on every occasion. What makes it hard is that, even when you may be able to see someone suffering, if it has been self-inflicted and yet the wider team are also made to suffer as a result of their action, as a leader one is not always able to remain neutral.

When I joined St Leonard's, I was aware of a relationship dispute that had existed for over a year. Many people had been involved in trying to bring it to a satisfactory conclusion within a spirit of Christian fellowship. However, neutrality in leadership clearly had not been working. My compassion was for the morale of the wider staff and for the children. Compassion is not soft. It is to be found at the heart of human suffering and therefore the act of showing compassion can be painful also. It's not always easy to generate, particularly if someone has let you down.

As a school leader, there will be several occasions where you find yourself in a moment feeling as if you have to choose between showing compassion for an individual or doing the right thing for the organisation. Whilst when removed from a situation you may *know* what needs to be done in the circumstance, actually *doing* it is not always easy. As a servant leader, have compassion but exercise wisdom and remember whom it is that you are actually serving.

### Forgiveness

Luke 23:34 outlines arguably the greatest act of forgiveness in the Bible. Jesus on the cross pleads, *"Father, forgive them for they know not what they do."* As he is making the ultimate sacrifice, he finds it within his heart to forgive his tormentors. When saying the Lord's Prayer, we petition God to *"forgive us our sins as we forgive those who sin against us."*

Being honest, as I hope I've portrayed myself throughout this book, this is an element of leadership which I find very challenging. But leadership for a Christian isn't meant to be any easier than it is for other leaders and it is important that your colleagues can see you *do* the right thing even if it takes time for it to *feel* right. The most important thing is to be really careful about who you allow yourself to become close to and then always be prepared to listen to their reflections carefully. An adage which resonates strongly for me is, *"Advice is something you ask for when you already know the answer but wish you didn't!"* I am not brilliant at being able to forgive by myself, but there are a few individuals who know how to help me and I'm not afraid to seek them out.

As a leader, it's important to understand that there are always consequences surrounding forgiveness. If you are habitually unable to forgive, then the truth is that your leadership will increasingly diminish. People will be afraid to take risks. They will be unable to share anxieties with you. They will not see you so much as a leader but as a "boss". Relationships will suffer, staff turnover is more likely to be high and your school is less likely to achieve great success.

Similarly, if you're seen to be very quick to forgive and forget absolutely everything and reluctant to enforce sanctions, whilst it may make you popular for a period, it is likely that people will lose faith in your ability to make difficult decisions and secure accountability.

As the saying goes, *"to err is human; to forgive, divine."* However, forgiveness is only one side of the coin. The other is trust. There are some occasions, when the very foundation of your working relationship may have been undermined, where you just need to get to the place where you're genuinely wishing someone well as you're parting ways, because you know that it is not going to be possible for you to continue working together in the same way. A friend of mine explains such a situation by describing someone as, *"A cracked mirror: he /she can still do a job for you, but you'll always be hoping to replace it."* I think this analogy describes the situation perfectly.

The associated chapter of *Leave A Light On* looks at the difference between friends and allies, the personal and the professional. Whilst love in a personal relationship is unconditional, trust in a professional relationship isn't. It's based on loyalty, ability, reciprocity and empathy. As a Christian leader of course, you are not left to only place your trust in others. Sometimes, a situation you're facing can be overwhelming and you may not wish to place a burden on someone else's shoulders – the *monkey on the back* as Andy Buck describes it. These verses from the Bible are perfect for such times.

*"Trust in the Lord with all your heart and lean not on your own understanding."* Proverbs 3:5

*"Cast your burden upon the Lord and he will sustain you; he will never let the righteous be shaken." Psalm 55:22*

Some questions which may help you with your reflection:

∞ Where is grace shown within your school?

∞ Who needs you to show grace at this time?

∞ Do you lead with empathy or sympathy?

∞ Whom do you trust?

∞ Who needs your forgiveness?

∞ What burden do you need to give over to God's grace?

# Fortune Favours

*"What you have said in the dark will be heard in the daylight, and what you have whispered in the ear in the inner rooms will be proclaimed from the roofs."*
**Luke 12:3**

Jesus' ministry, teaching and roaming throughout the Holy Land is thought to have lasted for up to three years. That Christianity grew so quickly into the world religion we know to today is testimony to Jesus' message and how it resonated with people. However, there is also an unquestionable fact which is often over-looked: He got by with a little help from his friends.

Jesus chose his closest followers very carefully. He needed people he could trust to send out his message and to continue the work when he was no longer around to lead the embryonic Christian movement. They were Jesus' most acquainted allies and companions.

### Jesus the delegator

As a church school leader, one needs to look no further than the New Testament for a guide to the art of delegation. Jesus makes his vision for the team clear: *"Follow me and I will make you fish for people." (Matthew 4:19)* He then spends quality time with his disciples, modelling the behaviours and approach that he wishes them to adopt. As an act of grace, he bestows his authority upon them, setting them up to succeed in the process. Finally, Jesus is not a micro manager. He puts his trust in his team prior to his ascension. Whilst he specifies in the passage below what was involved in going and making disciples of all nations, he doesn't dictate methodology and style for baptism or teaching.

*Then Jesus came to them and said, "All authority in heaven and on earth has been given to me. Therefore, go and make disciples of all nations, baptising them in the name of* the Father and of the Son and of the Holy Spirit, and teaching them to obey everything I have commanded you. And surely I am with you always, to the very end of the age." (Matthew 28:18-20)

Interestingly, Jesus also explains that the disciples will do their greatest work when he is no longer physically with them. He understood that knowing when to leave as the leader is also an important judgment to get right.

"Very truly I tell you, whoever believes in me will do the works I have been doing, and they will do even greater things than these, because I am going to the Father." John 14:12

A while later, we learn in chapter 3 of Acts that the disciples themselves have then learned the art of delegating when they choose Stephen and Philip to assist with food distribution whilst they concentrate on their ministry.

### Getting Results

Luke 11 describes Jesus teaching the disciples how to pray. It's where we are introduced to the words of the Lord's Prayer. However, it is not the case that the Church school leader is simply required to pray to get results. When Jesus exemplifies his teaching through a short parable, he talks of the *"shameless audacity"* required. The Greek word *anaideia* is used. This word implies both a sense of boldness and perseverance. It does not yield to pressure, discouragement, fear or exhaustion. Nor does it succumb to impatience. In verses 9 and 10, Jesus utters these well-known words: *"So I say to you: Ask and it will be given to you; seek and you will find; knock and the door will be opened to you. For everyone who asks receives; the one who seeks finds; and to the one who knocks, the door will be opened."* These words are an inspiration for the Christian leader and they also underline the importance of asking for help.

## The importance of faith

Luke 5 provides us with one of the most dramatic examples of *getting results*. The disciples have been fishing all night and caught nothing. Jesus says to Simon, *"Put out into deep water, and let down the nets for a catch."* Simon does as Jesus asks him and we are told, *"When they had done so, they caught such a large number of fish that their nets began to break. So they signalled their partners in the other boat to come and help them, and they came and filled both boats so full that they began to sink."*

Now it is important not to trivialise this story. It will not be the case that you can leave your *Good Level of Development* or your SATs results to a leap of faith. However, the Christian leader will know that whatever the outcome of individual circumstances, you will always have enough and be enough to lead your school if you believe and trust that you are leading with God's grace and blessing.

Some questions which may help you with your reflection:

∞ Are you creating followers or leaders?
∞ Why, when and what do you delegate?
∞ How are you preparing the school for life after your leadership?
∞ How do you show *shameless audacity?*
∞ How is God helping you to lead?

# Sailing West

*"The wind blows wherever it pleases. You hear its sound, but you cannot tell where it comes from or where it is going. So it is with everyone born of the Spirit."*
**John 3:8**

### All aboard

As the American jurist Oliver Wendell Holmes said, *"To reach a port we must sail, sometimes with the wind, and sometimes against it. But we must not drift or lie at anchor."* As school leaders, we cannot control the wind but must simply accept it. We are challenged to adjust to what is, to learn acceptance and work with what is given, to live in the world as it is, rather than wish for a world as it ought to be.

In a blog post, *Is your Spiritual Life like a Sailboat or a Motorboat?* (2013), Charles Pope, a Roman Catholic priest in Washington DC, explores the analogy between those who lead their lives as if in a motorboat compared with those in a sailing boat. He asserts that a Christian life involves choosing to be open to the will and breath of God (the wind) rather than being in the motorboat trying to control everything. He says:

*"We cannot control God, nor should we. Our role is to sense His direction and put out our sails accordingly. We are to "romance the wind" by growing deeper in our love and trust of God. We are to discover the serenity of accepting what is, of following the lead of God, or receiving what is offered rather than seeking to control and manipulate outcomes."*

This beautifully illustrates a nuanced difference between the expected leadership style of a Church school leader compared with other school systems. Certainly, the notion of *super head* is completely incompatible with leadership in Church schools.

## The Challenge of Jesus' Leadership Style

Jesus' example of leadership was radically different from the example in the world at that time. His approach should provide us with all the encouragement we need to challenge the educational landscape as it is.

Jesus' leadership style was neither about command and control, nor status and power. He was not so bothered about techniques and methods. Instead, he focused on developing character stemming from a Christ-like servant heart. He modelled servanthood and challenged his disciples to follow that example – to be like him.

One only has to look at the way politicians have lauded a few notable individuals within the world of education to understand that they believe that some who lead are in some way better than the people whom they lead. They gain status because they exercise power over others to achieve their goals. All of which leads to rewards, benefits and preferential treatment.

Jesus would certainly rebuke such an approach. In Matthew 23, he says:

*"But do not do what they do, for they do not practise what they preach. They tie up heavy, cumbersome loads and put them on other people's shoulders, but they themselves are not willing to lift a finger to move them…*
*The greatest among you will be your servant. For those who exalt themselves will be humbled, and those who humble themselves will be exalted."*

The goal of the Church school leader is to serve those whom we lead in a way that enables them to achieve the purpose which God has called them to. In the context of the Kingdom of God, our team are not the leader's tools but together, we collaboratively serve God and His purposes. This is the leadership style of Jesus.

## The importance of risk taking

If you want to succeed as a leader, then you have to be prepared to take risks at key moments. The word *risk* comes from the Italian *risco* meaning *danger*. It is defined in English as *to expose to danger or loss*. This is not to say that you are encouraged to become reckless or cavalier - to do so would obviously be foolish. Whilst the Bible contains stories where the faithful have made the ultimate sacrifice, it also contains stories such as Paul leaving Damascus in a basket where action is taken to preserve his life.

So, when should you take a risk and when should you opt for safety? The question which needs to be asked is, *"For what / whom are you prepared to take a risk?"* This links directly with your vision and values. Where in your philosophy and approach is there no room for compromise? As a Church school leader, you are called to trust that, if it is God's will, it will happen somehow and at some point. So, who are you leading for?

Some questions which may help you in your reflection:
- ∞ Are you leading in a sailboat or a motorboat?
- ∞ Whom do you serve?
- ∞ How are you serving others well in your leadership?
- ∞ What risk are you being called to take?

# Build Upon the Rock

*"You are a rock, and upon this rock I will build my church."*
**Matthew 16:18**

Jesus says the words above after Simon has declared Jesus to be the Messiah at a gathering of the disciples in Caesarea Philippi. For Simon Peter, to hear these words must have felt both a privilege and an awesome responsibility. The same is so for those fortunate enough to lead in a Church school. The Christian church has existed for two thousand years and you are playing your part in retelling the story and giving it meaning within your communities. The responsibility to build the Church is also now yours.

## The Church and its leaders

In Luke 6, we read the famous analogy of the wise and foolish builders building on rock and sand respectively. Our leadership is to be founded on the message of the gospel rather than the Department for Education. There will be times in your leadership journey when the pressures of the day will demand that you focus on meeting the requirements of the state. However, as a Church school leader you are always called to consider action in the light of the school's historical foundation. When there is conflicting pressure, that is when your leadership will be tested the most.

It's also important to remember that your leadership is never to be considered in the light of personal ambition. Not only will this lead you into strife with your colleagues, but it will also tempt you away from the purpose of your leadership. You are just one person in the history of your school. You have a duty to build well upon what is already there so that those coming after you inherit a job well done and can build upon your work. In Paul's first letter to the people of Corinth, he warns them about the dangers of ignoring the value of foundation. He tells them:

"By the grace God has given me, I laid a foundation as a wise builder, and someone else is building on it. But each one should build with care. For no one can lay any foundation other than the one already laid, which is Jesus Christ. If anyone builds on this foundation using gold, silver, costly stones, wood, hay or straw, their work will be shown for what it is, because the Day will bring it to light."

## Be Inspired

In the associated chapter of *Leave A Light On*, I challenge you to be inspired by your school's history. Build in the story of your church as well; it's foundation and history. However ancient or modern your church is, there will be some hidden gems to uncover which can bring the church's story alive for children. Connect your leadership with what has gone before and lay a firm foundation for what is yet to come.

Some questions which may help you in your reflection:
∞ How will you build Christ's church in your role?
∞ How connected is your school with the church?
∞ What are the foundations of your leadership?

# Hope Springs Eternal

*"But the path of the righteous is like the light of dawn, that shines brighter and brighter until the full day."*
**Proverbs 4:18**

### The importance of hope

The concept of hope has always been important to me as a teacher and school leader, and indeed as an individual. I have seen the consequences of the absence of hope in both children and adults and it's just about the most difficult thing to witness or experience.

Hope is defined as *"a feeling of expectation and desire."* One could argue that the hope expressed in our world today all too often is focused on our desires rather than our beliefs. This provides us with another nuanced understanding for the leader of the Church school.

### Biblical understanding of hope

Whilst I hope that Arsenal are successful every season, unfortunately for me, there is little evidence to suggest that I may expect this to happen. However, the hope spoken of in the Bible is that much greater because the Christian understanding of hope resides more in *expectation* rather than *desire*. There is an element of certainty to it which is lacking in the secular understanding of the word. Biblical hope not only yearns for a brighter future – there's an expectation that it will happen. Greater than this, there's a confidence that it will happen.

Psalm 42:5 includes the words *"Hope in God."* This is not asking you to *take a chance* or *keep your fingers crossed.* Rather it's a confident declaration that you should *expect* great things from God.

In the letter to Hebrews we read, *"God is not unjust; he will not forget your work and the love you have shown him as you have helped his people and continue to help them. We want each of you to show this same diligence to the very end, so that what you hope for may be fully realised." (Hebrews 6: 10-11)*

The verses above not only illustrate the importance of maintaining hope so that what has been promised may come to fruition, they also explain the importance of perseverance. The motto on the St Leonard's school badge is *Strive and Persevere.* Rather than looking upon this phrase as a somewhat dated image of an arduous pursuit of learning, it signposts the child to the certainty that, if they continue to try their very best, God's promise for them will be fulfilled. The Church school leader knows that, *"We have this hope as an anchor for the soul, firm and secure." (Hebrews 6:19)*

### What should a Church school leader hope for?

The Leadership Matters model lends itself perfectly to Christian leadership. In a Church of England school, there should be an expectation that your personal qualities will create a *culture* and *climate* which enables Jesus' promise of 'life in all its fullness' to be realised for all within your school community, children and adults alike. Should you be successful in this, whilst no one can expect for results to place you at the top of any league table every year (much like Arsenal!), one can expect there to be consistently high outcomes in terms of people – their dispositions and attitudes; their willingness to serve God and to serve others; their willingness to strive and persevere and their willingness to show the fruit of the spirit to stranger and neighbour alike.

At St Leonard's we often sing (and clap an ostinato!) *This Little Light of Mine.* The real hope and expectation for a Church school leader is that you, your team and your children promise that, *"where there's a dark corner in this land, I'm going to let my little light shine."* I wish you well in your leadership journey in the certain hope that, if you have been called, are connected and committed to leading for others, God's purpose for you will be realised.

# Reading and references

## Books

A Quiet Education – Jamie Thom (2020)

All I Need to Know I Learned in Kindergarten – Robert Fulghum (1988)

Basic Coaching – Andy Buck (2020)

Diary of a Young Girl – Anne Frank (1947)

Finding Your Element – Sir Ken Robinson (2013)

Good to Great – Jim Collins (2001)

Hopeful Schools – Mary Myatt (2016)

Imperfect Leadership – Steve Munby (2019)

Leadership Matters 3.0 – Andy Buck (2018)

Leadership Plain and Simple – Steve Radcliffe (2012)

Liminal Leadership – Stephen Tierney (2016)

Radical Candor – Kim Scott (2017)

Start with Why? – Simon Sinek (2009)

The Greats on Leadership – Jocelyn Davis (2016)

The Righteous Mind – Jonathan Haidt (2012)

The Speed of Trust – Steven Covey (2008)

## Models

Accountability Continuum – Andy Buck (2018)

Change curve – Elisabeth Kübler-Ross (1969)

Components of Trust – Steven Covey (2008) adapted

Courage and Resilience – Robertson Cooper

Delegation – Tim Brighouse (2007) Hay Group Model (2007)

Difficult Conversations – Susan Scott (2003)

Dimensions of change – Knoster, Thousand and Villa (2000)

Eight steps of change –John Kotter (1996)

Emotional Intelligence – Daniel Goleman (2000)

Formation of Strategy – Greenway, Blacknell and Coombe (2018)

Friends and Allies – Jocelyn Davis (2016)

International Primary Curriculum – Fieldwork Education (founded 2000)

Johari Window – Luft and Ingham (1955)

Managing individual performance – Pendleton and Furnham (2012) adapted by Andy Buck

Performance and Values – Pendleton and Furnham (2012)

Primary Colours - David Pendleton (2012)

Prioritisation – Eisenhower Matrix

School Improvement – Sir David Carter

Sigmoid curve – based on logistic function (1845)

Subject Leader monitoring – Simon Jackson (2020)

Team Development – adapted by Andy Buck based on Tuckman (1965) and Lencioni (2002)

Zone of Growth – Yerkes and Dodson (1908) adapted

## Other References

BBC Teach

Called Connected Committed – Church of England's Foundation for Educational Leadership, Ford and Wolfe (2020)

churchofengland.org

Composition of Teams – Will Greenwood from Daily Telegraph (2020)

Framework for Governance – National Governors' Association (2015)

Interview with Dr Lydia Jaeger – War Cry (2014)

Is your spiritual life like a sailboat or a motorboat? – Charles Pope (2013)

Leadership that gets results – Daniel Goleman (2000)

Statutory Inspection of Anglican and Methodist Schools (2018)

# Acknowledgements

**Those who have supported me with this book**

Andy Buck – This book is one big acknowledgement! Thank you.

Canon Anna Norman-Walker – For your help with this book. For brightening up all of our lives. For leading with faith, hope, love…and magic!

Laurielle Jackson – Both the beauty and the brains behind our operation. For all your expertise in supporting our EYFS and for your endless patience and support with both my headship and this book. Thank you. Headship is calling you!

Natasha Gavin – Words will never do your talent or your character justice. For transforming my Monday mornings. For keeping me sane. For your calm brilliance and understanding glances. For your help with this book. For being you. Thank you.

Paul White – For the *cracked mirror* analogy. Explained brilliantly and simply what I'd found so difficult to express.

## Other acknowledgements

All who have been part of the history and improvement journey within St Leonard's. This book is testament to your talent and dedication.

Amanda Chaloner – When you arrived, people saw the light and it's been undiminished ever since. A rock also. The Bergkamp of the teaching world. Thank you doesn't begin to say it.

Anne Doyle – For all that you enabled me to learn through books and for your wisdom. For your friendship and eternal optimism. This one's for you.

Colin Powell – El Presidente! For being brave enough to be part of the panel which appointed me and for your calm counsel ever since.

David James – So much more than a site manager.

IPC Personnel – The team at Fieldwork Education who've worked in partnership with St Leonard's.

Julie Brine – Integrity in heels. The only person I worked for twice. A lady and a great head teacher.

Lambeth School Leaders – Too numerous to mention, but too important to neglect.

Laura Akhtar – One more step to go. *The Chosen One.*

Lorraine Bell – "Don't get it right; get it written!" For opening teachers' eyes in those early days to the need for writing stamina. Your leadership mattered.

Mark Lawrence – For always being prepared to share the load and for being wise… with the help of a few pints.

Philip Jones – The calm in any storm. Wishing you a long, happy and healthy retirement.

Rev Mary Hawes – As Chair, you announced my appointment with champagne. I'm surprised it wasn't gin! I will always be grateful for you giving me the opportunity to lead at St Leonard's and it's always a pleasure to welcome you back.

Richard Blackmore – The best School Improvement Partner any new head could wish to have. Now an ally and a friend. Thank you.

Sarah-Anne Fernandes – Our maths journey has been the longest and most challenging to make. For your brilliance and support; thank you.

SDBE MAT – For all of your support as St Leonard's *sails west*.

SLT past & present – It's all about the team. Don't worry – we won't use this book for Book Club!

So many teachers, support staff and governors past and present – You are admired, respected and appreciated. The 2020 team – history will judge you well.

Sue Heeley – As Chair of Governors for 8 years, your support and advice was always appreciated, as was your chairing of meetings which started and ended on time! Thank you.

Tony Pizzoferro – Loyal and committed. A life of service. I was so fortunate to have you in post when I started. For 25 years' service to St Leonard's; thank you.